NORTHERN FINLAND'S POST-WAR

COLONIZING AND EMIGRATION

EUROPEAN DEMOGRAPHIC MONOGRAPHS

IV

Northern Finland's Post-War Colonizing and Emigration

A GEOGRAPHICAL ANALYSIS OF
RURAL DEMOGRAPHIC COUNTER-CURRENTS

by

KIRK H. STONE

Department of Geography and
Institute for Behavioral Research,
University of Georgia

SPRINGER-SCIENCE+BUSINESS MEDIA, B.V

To
the youngsters of Finland
who, like the youngsters of the world
— especially James Kevin, Jeffrey Kirk, and Melanie Grace —
are the objects of our thoughts, worries, hopes,
and pride
and for whom we labor to provide more
acceptable examples and an improved world.

Originally published by Martinus Nijhoff, The Hague, Netherlands in 1973

ISBN 978-90-247-1570-1 ISBN 978-94-010-2005-3 (eBook)
DOI 10.1007/978-94-010-2005-3

TABLE OF CONTENTS

LIST OF FIGURES

M = Map, P = Picture, G = Graph

LIST OF TABLES

FOREWORD

As the world's population increases, where will it live? Surely many will end up in cities for a recent United Nations' report anticipates that the globe's urban people will increase from 1.33 billion in 1970 to 3.09 billion in the year 2000. In the same period, however, the expectation is that rural population will increase from 2.25 billion to 3.02 billion. Of course the latter will be unevenly distributed; 91 per cent are likely to be in the less developed regions of the world while the rural folks of the more developed areas are expected to decline from 335 million to 255 million by 2000 A.D. No matter where, the major part of the increasing rural population probably will go to areas already thinly to densely settled. But not all.

Even in parts of the more developed nations and for sure in many of the less developed countries one may expect significant numbers of people to move to what is now uninhabited land. Why? Because this is the nature of people and of nations. Research on the subject discloses that new rural settling is not a limited action that is restricted areally or in time. Rather it is a natural and continuing process that evidences variety in a nation's desires; these may be expressed directly or indirectly by national governments through sponsored action or simply by permissiveness.

Accepting the Challenge

Ever since the 1930's the edges of the inhabited world have been a professional and personal challenge to me. It started simply from interest. At first there was a little dramatic quality – the "Go North, Young Man!" syndrome – but only a few field seasons provided sobering observations of either very hard work or unsuccessful or failing families. This seemed senseless in a sophisticated 20th-century world. My search in Alaska for guides to insure greater degrees of permanence in new rural settling appeared somewhat fruitless because of the recency of Alaskan settling. Extension of the effort to Canada provided many more examples and stimulated interest in planning for new rural settling. But things were still too new.

At this point in time the high latitudes appeared too restrictive for my needs. I not only wanted to put some "geo" back in Geography – that is, to go against the trend of intense specialization on small areas and limited topics – but, also, to increase the physical and cultural variables to be studied so as to seek guides that would save the potential wastes of people, time, and money in new rural settling. Deep penetration into the literature of rural settlement morphology and rural settling process plus occasional field forays into mid-latitude dry-land margins and low latitude tropical areas disclosed a repetition of elements of importance. It was clear that our planners had many useful techniques to conquer problems of natural origin – through different kinds of engineers (civil, mechanical, agricultural, and biological) problems of construction, drainage, cultivation, and animal strains could be solved.

But it was equally clear that our "human engineering" was weak. In fact, such elements as the methods of selecting settlers with high degrees of success appeared to be the "Achilles heel" of planning for new rural settling. At the same time this human engineering showed prerequisites needed from several disciplines in the social sciences (at least, psychology, sociology, anthropology, and economics). The geography of isolation became very clearly a central topic around which the complexities of interrelated physical and cultural elements revolved and could be analyzed at differing scales. A return to more detailed work in the Northern Lands then appeared in order; it was there that I had the advantages of prior experience, some regional similarities, varying degrees of isolation, and helpful contacts. And by moving the investigation to northern Europe the study of an area of old, rather than new, settlement was possible.

Norden

The contrast of settling processes operative in contemporary Scandinavia and Finland has been most instructive. In 1955, when we began work in Norden, Iceland was characterized by some spot abandoning of farms at its inhabited edges, Norway by spot advancing and stability of rural settlement, Sweden by retreat occurring on a regional scale in the north, and northern Finland by advancing on a regional scale. Analyses of the first three carried through a period of more spot retreating in Iceland, an end of spot advancing in Norway, and continued regional retreating in Sweden. Publication of the results led to the formulation of some guides to new rural settling. Comparison of these areas with other parts of the world led to the development of early measures of isolation which now appear applicable globally. It also led to recognition of the value of longer-time study of colonizing. Finland was selected for this because of its regional advancing of settlement, good documentary and cartographic records, and extremely helpful people. It was purely an accident in timing that work there went past the end of sponsored colonizing in Lapland Province and into the clash of the demographic counter-current of emigration. Though I am unhappy over the strains this caused in the population there I am grateful for the additional insights it provided into a great nation and a superior people. Seeing both during field work in 1955-56, 1958, 1959, 1960, 1964, and 1970 could not help but reduce some of my objectivity; it is difficult not to become emotionally involved with the Finns for it is so natural to admire their inner strength, to respect their balance, and to venerate their basic sense of values. As expressed in their national hymn their optimism about the future is a model for anyone:

Thy blossom, in the bud laid low
Yet ripened shall upspring.
See! From our love once more shall grow
Thy light, thy joy, thy hope, they glow!
And clearer yet one day shall ring
The song our land shall sing!

ACKNOWLEDGEMENTS

A foreigner working so long in so distant an area could never have completed this phase of his work without the support of numerous agencies and individuals. Especially in view of his linguistic weaknesses and the complexities of the oral and written Finnish language. I pay tribute to all and to selected ones here not only out of gratitude but also in order that others interested in following this line of research may know how to initiate their efforts efficiently.

The beginning of my work depended entirely on three agencies: the United States Educational Foundation (Fulbright Program) offices in Helsinki and Oslo, the Geography Branch of the Office of Naval Research in the U.S. Department of the Navy, and the University of Wisconsin. The Navy's sponsorship of a non-military, unclassified, basic research grant for four years was the major impetus and its administration by Dr. Louis O. Quam and Miss Evelyn L. Pruitt was exceedingly helpful. All through the study officials in Helsinki and in the regional centers of the Colonization Office and the General Survey Office were constantly and fully cooperative. In Helsinki, too, colleagues in the Geographical Institutes at the three major universities gave willingly of their time and effort. The more recent work was made possible by the University of Georgia, by a research grant from the American Council of Learned Societies for the 1970 field season, and by special cooperation of the Central Statistical Bureau in Helsinki.

Individuals who aided are truly in the hundreds – there was always someone to keep me from faltering badly. My Vera went far beyond the usual wifely aids and never gave up helping in spite of mosquitos, the midnight sun, dusty roads, and the perils of shopping by way of Finnish labels. Field assistance was faithfully and generously given by Dr. Hans Aldskogius and Fil. Mag. Kurt-Viking Abrahamsson and backing during office analyses was made pleasant and productive by Melvin H. Aamodt, James R. Carter, Samuel W. Putney, and John Tuck, Jr. Those special Finns who somehow always found a way for me are: Chief Jorma Hyppölä of the Central Statistical Bureau, Professor and Mrs. K. U. Pihkala of the University of Helsinki, Maiestris Heikki and Ritva Salonen of Tapiola, the late Professor Helmer Smeds, and Agronom Paavo Vainio of Rovaniemi. To the very capable and renowned editor of this series, Dr. Gunther Beijer of The Hague, goes my appreciation for encouragement and example over the years. Here at home two who became quite indispensable are Mrs. Brooke B. Wisdom and Mr. James D. Ingram, the former for patience and accuracy while typing such as the 30-letter Finnish names and the latter for consistantly top-quality cartographic design and delineation in the University of Georgia's Cartographic Services Laboratory. Most numerous and often closest to the heart are the many settlers throughout middle and northern Finland who granted so much hospitality and who patiently tried to teach me about new rural settling and emigration as well as – with somewhat less success – the proper use of the sauna.

Chapter 1

A PRELIMINARY SUMMARY

> "The population density of an area, its carrying capacity, depends mainly not on its natural resources, but on the inhabitants' ability to make use of those resources. . . . There is a special word in Finnish, *sisu*, denoting a resolute determination to finish a given task however hard it be. The sisu has no doubt been fostered by pioneering work continuing for centuries in unusually hard conditions."
>
> Helmer Smeds in *A Geography of Norden*

Finland has long been an exemplary nation. Many people have admired its demonstrations of financial integrity, its military effectiveness, its ability to coexist peacefully with the Soviet Union on one side and democratic nations on the other; not a few have respected its contemporary economic viability earned in the face of overwhelming odds, and still others its modern urban planning and development.

Presently, though, northern Finland's Lapland Province warrants special attention. This is because the area has become a demographic model of opposing forces (Fig. 1), each of which is a most profitable subject of study.

New Rural Settling

On the one hand the province has experienced a strong post-World-War-II in-migration. At first an emergency by-product of the war, the encouragement of new rural settling later became a nationally-sponsored action.[1] People, all Finns and nearly half displaced persons, came in from three easterly directions and settled all over the southern half of the province. New farms and homesites were created in forests and on swamps, some as single places by individual families and some by groups of families to form colonies. Of the latter some 61 were formed between 1946 and 1971 comprising 1528 families. Thus, a total of about 7500 people was added to Lapland's population in just the colonies started in the past quarter century.

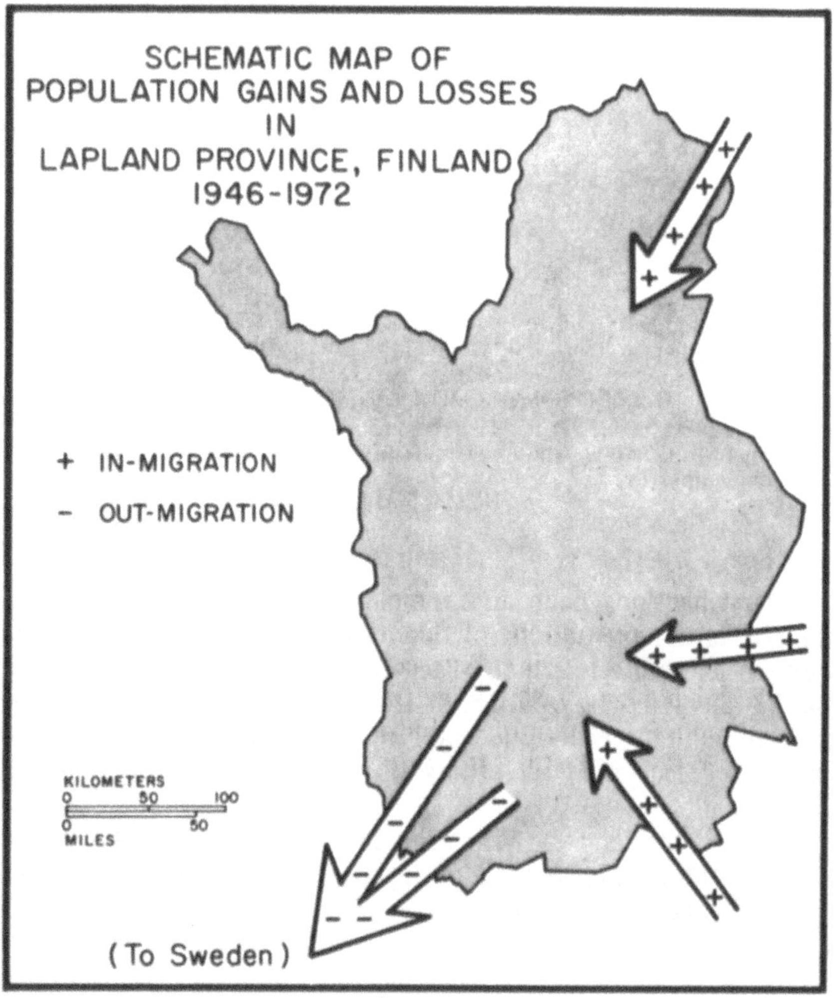

Figure 1

Within the colonies the range in characteristics is great. All have a moderate degree of regional isolation but varying degrees of local isolation for some adjoined already-cleared land and highways while others did not (Fig. 2). Most were started between 1946 and 1950 but two still have major initial clearing and construction under way. The range in families per colony is 5 to 101, in size from 676 to 12,066 hectares (1670 to 29,816 acres), and in arable land per farm and forest per farm at least 32 and 140 hectares (79 and 346 acres) respectively. Farming-forestry was the principal starting occupation with the raising of milk cattle dominant on the agricultural side, but recently small farms have been discouraged by governmental decrees. The result of all these is a contemporary mixed picture of some colonies appearing to be quite viable while others are clearly weak in details of at least geography, sociology, and economics so they are, therefore, lacking in degree of permanence.

Emigration

In opposition to the growth by colonization is a loss in Lapland's population. This is a recent subtraction as a result of emigration southwestward to Sweden (Fig. 1). The trend since 1956 has been predominantly of young males to industrial work and in 1969 and 1970 its force was strengthened by the Finnish government's discouragement of small farming.

Historically Finnish emigration to Sweden has been common. At times the higher standard of living has been attractive, at other times Sweden's neutrality, and at still others the availability of work; these coupled with occasional periods of economic depression within Finland resulted in areas of Finnish nationals settled permanently in Sweden (and some in Norway as well). The numbers of emigrés in recent centuries fluctuated considerably but in the early part of the 20th there were only 3500-5500 Finns residing in Sweden in any year. But in the decade following 1945 Finland's net emigration, nearly all to Sweden, was more than 10,000 persons per annum in two years.

Population losses became critical in the 1960s. Net Finnish migration, nearly all to Sweden, was estimated as 17,000 in 1965 but in 1969 Finns going to Sweden were measured as more than 38,000. By then, too, Finland's total population was declining.

The trend continued into the early 1970s but has now slackened. About 45,000 Finns emigrated in 1970 with monthly maxima in March and September. In April 1971 out- and in-migration balanced but emigrés were somewhat in excess again in the fall of 1971. In November 1971 the country's total population declined further; it has remained at a little more than 4,600,000 since December 1971 and national in-migration has exceeded that outwards. Population decline in a small country which is the only representative of the democratic world adjoining the Soviet Union is a serious issue at both international and provincial scales.

Within Lapland, however, population trends have been somewhat different. The 20 years following 1945 was a period of continual gains in population. Then rural losses began in 1966 and continued through

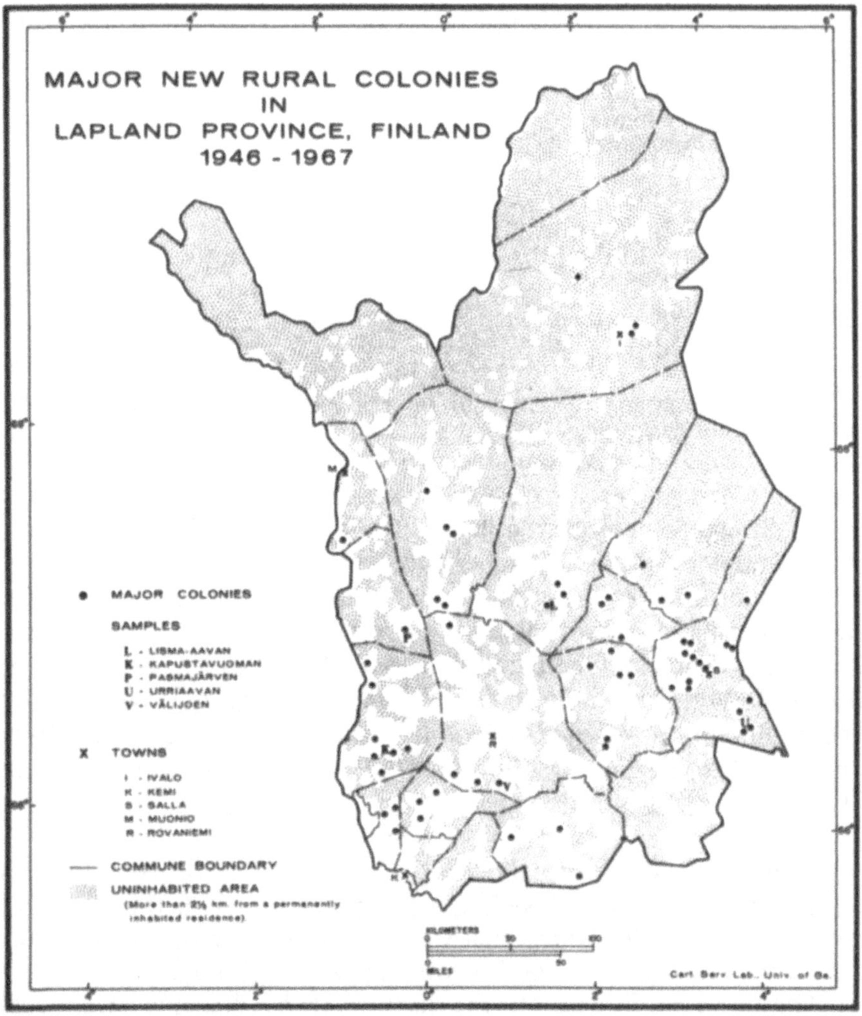

Figure 2

1970. The 1970 and 1971 losses, the first years of specific measurements, were the second greatest of all Finnish provinces. Maximum drops paralleled the national ones in time, being 750-900 per month in the fall of 1970 and generally somewhat less than 100 a month from August through October 1971. Oulu Province, just south of Lapland, had greater losses in total numbers but similar ones in time. Still the issue remains unsettled; although the national trend of excess migration (and that of Oulu Province) stopped in late 1971, Lapland had two months when there were more emigrants than immigrants early in 1972. Much population dynamism remains in the province.

In general it is certain that more Finns left Lapland for Swedish industry from 1966 through 1970 than came in for group colonizing in the past 25 years. Gains from the latter of roughly 7500 people were nearly canceled out in 1970 alone by a rural Lapland loss of 6100. And, it should be remembered, the four previous years was the time of near-maximum losses in the whole nation. Though this simple gain-loss relationship emphasizes a negative point there are also three positive ones: 1) the colonists' families have grown in size since their arrival, 2) the area of rural settlement expanded geographically and remained so, and 3) the processes of new rural settling – the principal point of inquiry herein – demonstrate a means of absorbing increased numbers of people. There is no question but that expansion of the ecumene could start again in Northern Finland.

Questions

Such opposing streams of additions and losses of population as have flowed across northern Finland during the past quarter century raise fundamental questions. The principal geographic ones are: 1) why and how did the settlers locate themselves where they did and 2) why did the emigrants leave the area where they were? Of course, such locational decisions are complex – people seldom locate for a single simple reason. Rather, the decisions are products of planned and intuitive thought of officials, of conscious and sub-conscious ideas and hopes of settlers, of national- or regional- or local-scale requirements and possibilities. All is made more complicated by varying degrees of emotional actions and reactions and the fact that an individual's aspirations and desires change with the passage of time. So one may summarize Lapland's recent experiences with prior recognition of probable over-simplification because of incomplete data.

The origin of the new rural settling forces was a single element. By the Treaties of Moscow (March 1940) and of Paris (February 1947) Finland ceded three eastern sectors to the Soviet Union: Karelia on the south, Salla-Kuusamo in the middle-north, and Petsamo in the far north. Finns in these areas could have stayed but they chose not to do so and moved generally westward into Lapland from a strong feeling of national loyalty. Why they picked the region of northern Finland is relatively clear for only those in the Salla-Kuusamo sector who were familiar with it. And why they went to particular colonies was only partly because of what was available at the time of movement (and this because of prior decisions by government officials on the expeditious acquisition of farm-forest land). Further, why certain families went to specific parcels is supposed to have originated with family or other social ties and is generally not recorded. Unfortunately many of these decisions at such different geographic, psychologic, economic, and sociologic levels and scales had to be made hurriedly. Later some decisions were revised. But some could not be.

The recent emigration of Laplanders (and others) was equally complex. The original attraction was relatively large and rapid increase of income in Sweden. But a foreign attraction is stronger only when the local attraction is weaker. One must ask: why do Finns, usually very nationalistic, leave at all; why do farmer-foresters go to industrial occupations; do northern Finns move to just any place in Sweden; do they go to any industry regardless of type? Or, is the migration intentionally impermanent? Or, has the ecumene been overextended northward in Finland and is this the first stage of contraction because of reduced governmental subsidies and, eventually, uneconomic occupational possibilities?

Answering these questions in all aspects for Lapland is a significant scientific goal. But fascinating as it is it is hardly attainable. As usual this study has generated far more questions than answers. But any clue to insure the permanence of new rural settling, or to point out its inadvisability, is worth the effort.

NOTES TO CHAPTER 1

1. The Geographical Society of Finland, *Suomi, A General Handbook on the Geography of Finland,* Helsinki, 1952; R. R. Platt (ed.), *Finland and Its Geography,* New York, 1955; W. R. Mead, *Farming in Finland,* London, 1953; H. Smeds, Finland, in A. Sømme (ed.), *A Geography of Norden,* Oslo, 1960, pp. 149-202; J. G. Gräno, Gehofte and Siedlungen in Finland, *Fennia,* v. 63, 1937, pp. 1-66; R. Kalliola, Man's Influence on Nature in Finland, *Fennia,* v. 85, 1961, pp. 9-23; H. Smeds, The Distribution of Urban and Rural Population in Southern Finland 1950, *Fennia,* v. 81, 1957, pp. 1-21; The Geographical Society of Finland, *Suomen Kartasto* (Atlas of Finland), Helsinki, 1960, plates 16 and 17; S. Jaatinen and W. R. Mead, The Intensification of Finnish Farming, *Economic Geography,* v. 33, 1957, pp. 31-40; I. Hustich, Finland, ett Utvecklat och ett Underutvecklat Land, *Meddelanden fran Ekonomisk-Geografiska Institutionen vid Svenska Handelshögskolan,* Helsingfors, Nr. 24, 1964, especially Fig. 8 on p. 37; and E. Ehlers, Das Ende der Agrar-kolonisation in Finnland, *Geographische Rundschau,* v. 22, 1970, pp. 31-33.

Chapter 2

GENERAL FINNISH POPULATION AND SETTLEMENT CHARACTERISTICS, 1946-1969

From the famine years of the 1860s to a maximum in 1969 Finland's population more than doubled. Growth, however, was at reduced rates. There were 2 million people in 1879, 3 million by 1908 (29 years), and 4 million in 1946 (38 years). In the quarter century after World War II growth continued to decelerate until the greatest number of 4.7 million was reached at the end of 1969. By contrast Lapland's numbers increased at much faster rates after 1946, a result of colonizing and rebuilding, but reached their highest figure by 1966. Thus, while the Continuous Settlement Region, the southern third of Finland, was urbanizing rapidly and losing some rural folk the Middle Fringe Zone of settlement in southern Lapland was changing somewhat similarly but undergoing major gains and then losses during the same period. So the pre-1946 changes in the geography and demography of Finland extended into the contemporary period.

Changes in Population Numbers, 1946-1969

In 1946 some inherited problems in population numbers were still in effect. One was adjustment to the loss of some 79,000 soldiers killed in combat. Another was an unknown number of missing civilian and military persons. Third were the displaced persons (DP). These were the 420,000 people who chose to move into Finland as a result of the ceding of the four Finnish areas to the Soviet Union by way of the Treaty of Moscow, dated March 1940, and again (after recapture) in the Treaty of Paris signed in February 1947. The three main sectors were on the eastern border: Karelia at the southern end, Salla-Kuusamo in the middle north, and Petsamo at the northern end. Almost all residents of these lands refused Soviet citizenship; there were 10,812 persons in the two northern sectors alone who moved mostly to Lapland province.[2] Lastly, a fourth trend was national growth.

From 1946 to 1969 the total number of Finns continued to increase. But the rate declined. Until 1956 there was a period of slower increase than in pre-war years, still slower growth then characterized the years to 1964, after which population increase dropped to its 1969 end (Fig. 3).

The post-war era began with about 4 million people in Finland. In the 1950 census some 4,030,000 were enumerated. This was a significant number because it represented the country's first direct general census, prior counts commonly being based on total enrollments in all church and civil registers.

By 1960 the country had 4,446,000. Compared to the 1950 total the average growth rate per year was a low 0.9% which changed, as noted above, in about 1956. Then during the next five years the total declined further so that in 1965, after a second break in rate, the total was 4,596,000. A falling birth rate (22.1/1000 in 1950 to 16.7/1000 in 1965) and emigration were taking effect.[3] And this slowing of growth kept on through 1969 when Finland's maximum total population was 4.7 millions.[4] Since then is the first time the country's total population declined under non-war conditions since the famine of 1866-1868.

In Lapland population development after 1946 differed from the national trend. The northern province increased at much greater rates through 1965. For example, its mean values for five year periods from 1951 through 1965 were: for population, 175, 195, and 213 thousands; the provincial changes per 1000 persons of these means, in comparison to the national changes, were 19.9 to 11.4, 21.9 to 9.6, and 14.2 to 7.9.[5] Thus, between 1951 and 1965 Lapland grew roughly twice as fast as all Finland. Colonizing contributed greatly to this.

Figure 3

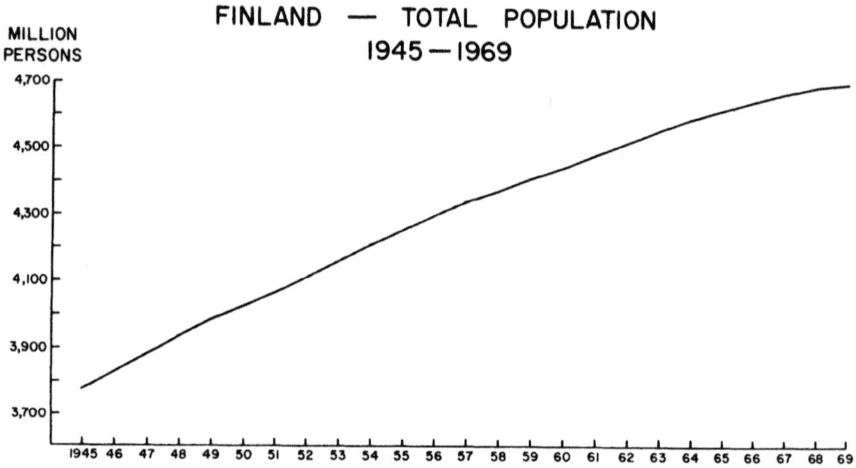

In 1966 population in the province peaked. About 221,000 persons were present and during the next two years the total declined less than 1000. Thereafter, however, decline was clearly the trend through the 1970 population of 217,581 and was forecast to continue (as noted in Chapter 5).[6]

Changes in Population Distribution, 1946-1969

While the number of people was changing so were the areal distributions. At first, between 1946 and 1969 the displaced persons increased both urban and rural populations and then colonizing continued in the north while urbanizing took place everywhere.

At the opening of the contemporary period three geographic generalizations applied to Finnish population. 1) Most of the people were in the southern part, 2) most of the people were on or quite near water, and 3) most were at lower elevations. These statements apply to all of Norden; in Finland they are specifically tied to prehistoric settlement in southwestern centers, a spread over the southern fifth of the nation and the Bothnian coast by 1550, and further extension northward over most of the country and the southwestern quarter of Lapland by 1640.[7] Thus, by 1946 the southern third of Finland was continuously settled in an areal sense and included the country's main cities. The dominance population-wise of this region is shown in that Finland's mean point of total population remains in Koskenpää commune, near Jyväskylä, where it has been from 1910 through 1960.[8]

This southern region absorbed most of the displaced persons immediately after World War II. A total of more than 420,000 left the four areas ceded (including Porkkala, west of Helsinki, where about 5800 were shifted even though the area was returned to Finland later). In an evacuation phase in 1944 and a resettling one in 1946 and 1947 the DPs moved to cities and rural areas, in the latter some settling on unused but cleared land and some on uncleared land ("cold farms").[9] It was this resettling of large numbers of people that resulted in second and more recent maxima of rural populations in southern Finland which probably would not have occurred otherwise. Still the action was responsible for increased rural densities and city sizes.

By 1946, too, a strong urbanizing trend had set in. Whereas in 1930 and 1940 only 18% and 23% of the people lived in cities and towns it went to about 32% by 1950, to more than 40% in 1960, to about 49% in 1968. From 1950 to 1965 increase in urban communes was steady but rural communes either slowed down or decreased and the losses were especially notable in rural communes with less than 6000 people.[10] Stated differently, the year of the first regional culmination of rural population was in 1910 or 1920 in most of the southern quarter of Finland with a northeastern and Bothnian fringe of 1950 and the remainder post-1960.[11] This meant urbanizing which did not, however, leave its mark on the landscape in the form of unusual numbers of vacant or abandoned homes. Cartographically the population of the southern half of Finland looked in 1967[12] quite similar to its appearance in 1950[13] with the exception of some increases in rural densities and considerable growth in the larger cities.

But such was not the case in Lapland. There colonizing was responsible for additions in the early part of the contemporary period of 7500 to perhaps 10000 DPs from the two ceded northern sectors. Also, there were some Karelian farmers who elected to move to Lapland. The greater part of this action was by groups of families, forming colonies, most of which were the "cold farm" type. Major colonies in the province numbered 61 and provided for 1528 families (as noted in Chapter 4) which included about 7500 people. Their settling had to be quick, without much prior organized experience, in a relatively large and discontinuously settled area, and under economic conditions that were strained by unreasonable war reparation requirements of the Soviet Union. Though the settling originally was for DPs several early additions included war soldiers, war

Figure 4. Middle Kemi River, Discontinuous Settlement Region. (See p. 93).

widows, and war invalids. As time passed the requirements for colonization were relaxed somewhat, indicating the government's desire to encourage new rural settling in the north by both colonies as well as by individual families on single farms. In short, Finland wanted its north colonized and worked hard at it.

These additional people caused supplements to the population maps at all scales. Regionally there were extensions northward of lines of inhabited areas along the major streams (Fig. 4) and roads. Sectionally there was a thickening of areas already settled when colonizing started, and in southern Lapland and adjoining Oulu Province there were distinct advances of the ecumene into unpopulated areas between the big rivers. Further, at the local scale new buildings and farms were introduced all over the region and the few cities grew very rapidly, especially percentagewise because of their small numerical bases.

These patterns are clear on the major new map of Finland's population.[14] Within Lapland four major north-south lines follow the principal rivers. Further, in the northernmost section there are numbers of spots of population and in the southernmost many groups of clusters and short and long lines. In this southern section, also, are the principal cities of Rovaniemi (29,700 people) and Kemijarvi (6600). In the adjoining province of Oulu on the south the people are in larger groups of clusters and even some uninterrupted areas while the two major centers are the cities of Kemi (32,200) and Kuusamo (5000).

These distributions were established by 1966 when the maximum population of the province was achieved. Still, of particular interest is the fact that the provincial losses of population since then were not apparent in vacant and abandoned rural homes in 1970. Thus the distributional patterns are holding geographically while losses are taking place demographically. Such changes reflect southern Lapland's position as part of the Middle Fringe Zone of Finland's Discontinuous Settlement Region. These are usually dynamic areas.

Regions and Zones of Settlement

Finland is at the northern edge of the inhabited world. This, its great north-south extent of 1100 km. (683 mi.), and its closed border next to the Soviet Union means that there is great variation in the dynamism of Finnish settlement. One means of understanding the difference is by measures of isolation. Recognizing and mapping them delineates areas of similar nature with respect to inter-regional and local access. Such knowledge is basic in analyzing the geographic and demographic qualities of rural settlement.

Three primary measures of isolation are employed here. They are: 1) the number of neighbors within minimal straight-line distances, 2) the number of transport routes near enough to a home to be used for shipment of materials in and products out of a region, and 3) the number of local transport routes available between neighbors (Table 1).

MEASURES OF ISOLATION

REGION, ZONE, TYPE	POPULATION DISTRIBUTION PATTERN	NUMBER OF ROUTES PROVIDING ACCESS*								SYNTHESIS: RELATIVE DEGREE OF ISOLATION	
		RAILROAD		ROAD		WATER		AIR			
POLEWARD		INTER-REGIONAL	LOCAL	INTER-REGIONAL	LOCAL	INTER-REGIONAL	LOCAL	INTER-REGIONAL	LOCAL	REGIONAL	LOCAL
UNPOPULATED	None (No population)	0	0	0	0	0	0	0	0	Very High	Very High
DISCONTINUOUS SETTLEMENT											
4. Outermost Fringe Zone	Spots									Very High	High
Inland Type		0	0	0	0	0	0-1s	0	0		
3. Outer Fringe Zone	Clusters of Spots, Occasional Short Lines										
Inland Type		0	0	0	1-2	0	0-1s	0	0-1	High	Moderate
Coastal Type		0	0	0	1-2s	0-1	1-3	0	0-1s		
2. Middle Fringe Zone	Groups of Clusters, Short and Long Lines									Moder-ate-Low	Low-Mod-erate
Inland Type		0-1	1-2	0-1	2-3	0	0-1s	0-1	0-1		
Coastal Type		0-1	0-1	0-1	1-3	1-3	1-4	0-3	0		
1. Inner Fringe Zone	Interrupted Areas, Clusters of Groups										
Inland Type		0-2	0-2	0-2	3-4	0	0-3s	0-1	0-1	Low	Low
Coastal Type		0-2	0-3	0-2	3-4	1s	1-4s	0-3	0-1		
CONTINUOUS SETTLEMENT	Uninterrupted Areas	1-2	2-4	1-3	3-4	0-3	0-4	0-3	0-4	Very Low	None

*—*Within approximately 10-20 English miles of each permanent resident.*
S—*Only summer access on some or all routes.*

The first measure is of the proximity of a settler to neighbors with respect to the supply or procurement of emergency or short-time aid. Assumptions are that such help must be no more than one hour's foot-travel time away and that throughout the seasons the average speed in that hour is five kilometers (3 mi.; of course, this is modified by the use of transport aids, such as, skis or bicycles and the presence of communication equipment). The measure is the number of major directions to a maximum of six (from central-place theory) from any residence to other homes within five kilometers by direct measures. The cartographic view of this is obtained by drawing circles on a map with 2 1/2-km. (1 1/2-mi.) radii centered at every permanently occupied residence. Where the resulting pattern is one of individual spots (under Population Distribution Pattern on Table 1) no one is close enough to reach any home within an hour so the places are said to have a maximum degree of local isolation as well as a maximum degree of discontinuity of settlement. If the pattern is one of narrow lines then settlers in each house, excepting end homes, might be aided from two directions. In clusters a few of the inner residences might be reached from up to six major directions and in an ascending order of size of agglomeration the number of such houses increases through groups of clusters, to interrupted areas, to a maximum of uninterrupted areas which are tens of kilometers in size.

The other two measures reflect a dwelling's accessibility by means other than on foot. This is determined by the number of inter-regional and local transport routes, going in different directions, that are within 16 to 32 km. (10 to 20 mi.) of a home (a distance determined empirically in several Continuous Settlement Regions). Thus, a home that is close to only one local railroad and one local road is said to have a measurably greater degree of regional and local isolation than a dwelling equally close to one inter-regional and one local railroad and one inter-regional and two local roads. All transport routes are classified as inter-regional or local types in order to specifically designate the former as generally all-weather lines over which bulky or heavy goods may be moved directly, quickly, and regularly into or out of a Discontinuous Settlement Region; the maximum number of these directions applying to transport routes is taken to be four.

Combining these measures leads, first, to a designation of settlement regions. Their minimum sizes are usually 200-300 km. (124-186 mi.) in both major directions in order to provide small-scale mapping of large areas so as eventually to obtain worldwide comparability. The three regions recognizable are: 1) Continuous Settlement where there is no local or regional isolation, 2) Discontinuous Settlement where there are variations in both kinds of isolation[15] from low to very high, and 3) Unpopulated in which there are neither permanent habitations nor, usually, fixed transport facilities.

Within the Discontinuous Settlement Region four fringe-of-settlement zones are discernible. These are combinations of relative degrees of regional and local isolations (Table 1, Synthesis column) and the four zones are named according to their distances away from the Continuous Settlement Region. Thus, the Inner Fringe Zone with minimum isolations usually adjoins the Continuous Settlement Region while isolations are higher and distances from Continuous Settlement are greater as one goes through the Middle, Outer, and Outermost Fringe Zones.

Finland's Continuous Settlement Region is its southern third. There settlement is oldest, permanent residences are densest, transport lines are most numerous and run in the most directions, farming-forestry is most continuous areally, and most of the country's main urbanized areas are present (Fig. 5). [16] There is even one area of abandoning.[17]

The remaining northern two-thirds of the country is the Discon-

Figure 5. The Continuous Settlement Region of Southern Finland. *(See p. 93).*

tinuous Settlement Region. In its southernmost part is the Inner Fringe Zone, mostly along the Baltic Sea coast, and the northern extremity is a mixture of Outer and Outermost Fringe Zones. The former is predominantly rural with interrupted areas of residences within 5 km. (3 mi.) of each other but the two northern zones represent widest spacings of homes, lowest frequencies of transport lines and, therefore, highest degrees of regional and local isolations.[18]

In between is the Middle Fringe Zone. It is the center of attention here because it is a belt 200-265 km. (124-165 mi.) wide extending NW/SE across southern Lapland (Fig. 6) in which the demographic cross-currents have mixed. Views of its details regarding distribution of permanently occupied homes and the types of transport provide major reasons for the dynamism of its demography since 1946.

Throughout the Middle Fringe Zone settlement is geographically quite discontinuous. Although the earliest modern-day inhabitants came in the late 16th and early 17th centuries most of the population increase took place in the 20th. In general these people built homes so that the major distributional pattern of inhabited areas is groups of clusters interspersed with some long and short lines as well as, in the northern part of the zone, some spots (Fig. 7). Probably half of its area is uninhabited (largely in public ownership) but the individual unoccupied parcels are quite irregular in shape and varied in size; in southern sections they are roughly 6 by 35 km. (4 by 22 mi.) and scattered but in the northern parts are four or five times larger and primarily in drainage divide areas.

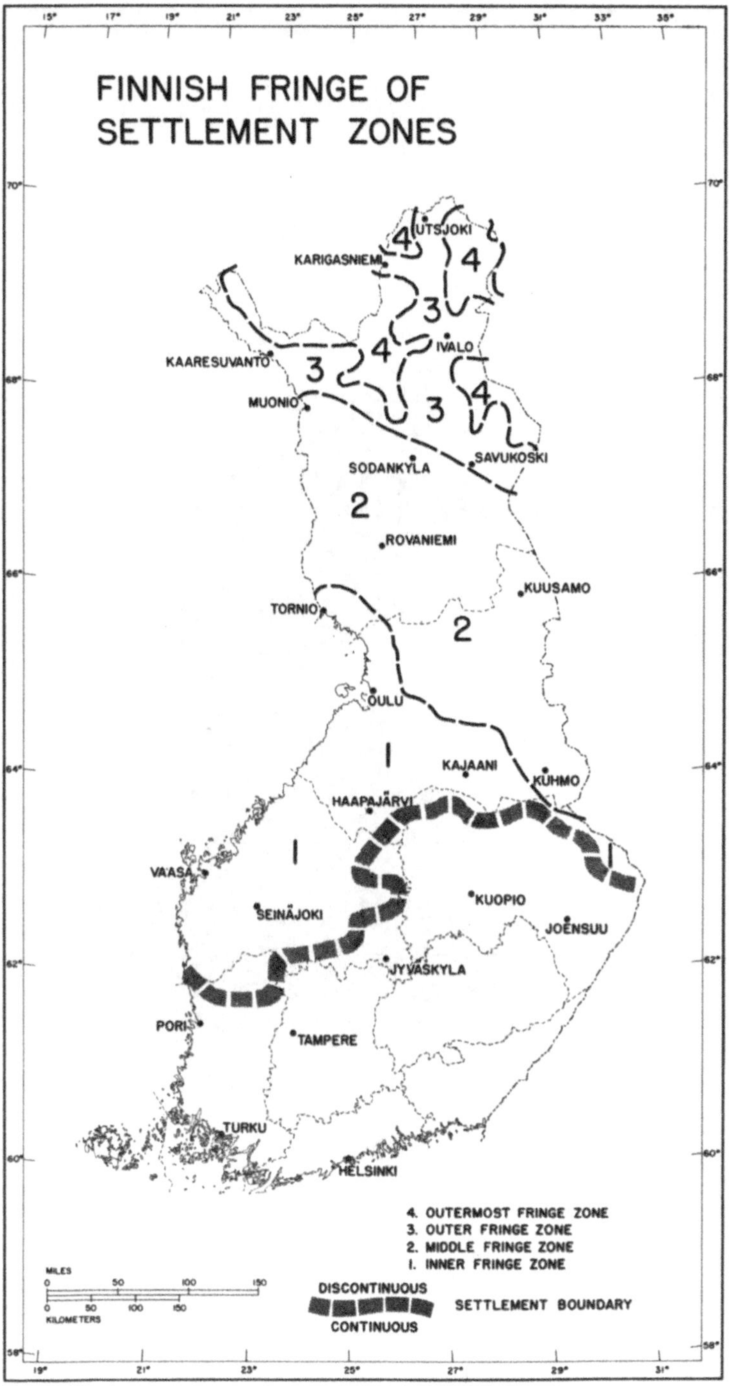
FINNISH FRINGE OF
SETTLEMENT ZONES
UTSJOKI
KARIGASNIEMI
IVALO
KAARESUVANTO
MUONIO
SAVUKOSKI
SODANKYLA
ROVANIEMI
KUUSAMO
TORNIO
OULU
KAJAANI
KUHMO
HAAPAJÄRVI
VAASA
KUOPIO
SEINÄJOKI
JOENSUU
JYVÄSKYLA
PORI
TAMPERE
TURKU
HELSINKI
4. OUTERMOST FRINGE ZONE
3. OUTER FRINGE ZONE
2. MIDDLE FRINGE ZONE
1. INNER FRINGE ZONE
MILES
KILOMETERS
DISCONTINUOUS
SETTLEMENT BOUNDARY
CONTINUOUS

Figure 6.

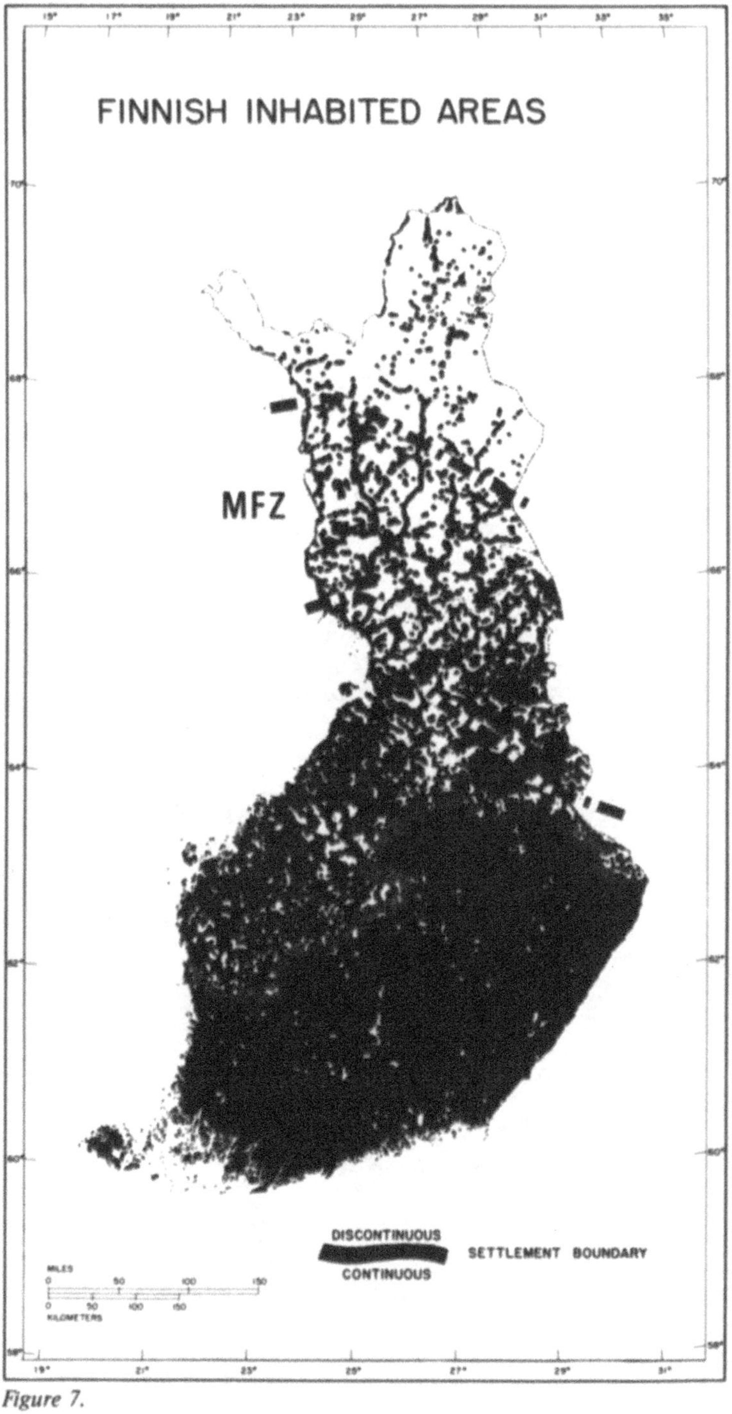
FINNISH INHABITED AREAS
MFZ
DISCONTINUOUS
CONTINUOUS
SETTLEMENT BOUNDARY
MILES
KILOMETERS
Figure 7.

The zone suffered severe losses in the 1940s. Destruction was widespread in conjunction with Finnish-Soviet clashes. Then Nazi withdrawal northward was marked by methodical destruction of nearly all buildings and bridges in Lapland. Many of these were being replaced at the beginning of the contemporary period, also the time of relocating westward of the displaced persons from the Salla-Kuusamo and Petsamo sectors. The 1940s were indeed busy years in Lapland.

Accessibility also began to change then. Not only did old lines need to be reopened but new ones had to be built for the colonies. The result is that the zone's regional and local isolations are moderate to low and are slowly becoming less. Only one railroad extends into Lapland and just two into the zone (Fig. 8). On them only local passenger service is available, mostly by daily rail buses, but they connect with inter-regional lines at Kemi and Kontiomaki. On the Lapland line passengers may go northeastward only as far as Kemijärvi but freight trains continue to Salla; construction of this route the rest of the way to the Soviet border was a treaty requirement but it can not be used east of Salla, and some rails on the Soviet side of the border (all mined and guarded from elevated observation posts) have been removed from the ties. Thus, rail accessibility is quite limited in the zone.

Lapland's major lessening of its isolations is by roads (Fig. 9). Two inter-regional highways, Nos. 4 and 21, cross its western part and one, No. 5, runs into the eastern part. They are standard E-route (major European road) width, black-topped or bound gravel, maintained regularly, and open all year. Most others are classed as local because they are two-cars wide (some less and with passing points), graveled loosely, and often broken at rivers where ferries provide the only crossing. At these points delays are common, in spring and fall because of the presence of moving ice and in summer because of the floating of logs to mills at river mouths. The many dead-end roads in the zone commonly are maintained by local agencies, have only dirt or loose gravel surfaces, and are usually one-car wide with widely spaced passing points. All roads, of course, stop at the Soviet border across which there is no traffic of any kind in the Middle Fringe Zone.

But even by road access for settlers differs. In the southern part of the zone most residents' homes are within 10-20 km. (6-12 mi.) of roads going in three or four directions. However, in the northern third one must travel farther for alternate routes, a few settlers are not immediately adjacent to a road, and some routes are closed occasionally. Yet roads in the more heavily settled sections have frequent truck and traveling-store service and most settlers are less than 25 km. (15 mi.) from daily bus service to a town; reaching a bus route by bicycle, motorcycle or spark (a chair-type sled) over this distance is accepted as a necessity by most of the zone's residents.

In addition there is airplane service at two points. Rovaniemi is connected to Helsinki by flights with stops at Kemi or Oulu. Across Lapland northward near-daily service is provided to Kirkenes, Norway with stops at Ivalo. At Rovaniemi charter flights may be originated to all parts of the province.

Further, there is a telephonic network. This is generally considered to be an emergency service in most of the zone. Different than in Sweden, each individual home is not likely to have an instrument but every major concentration of dwellings usually includes at least one phone and at more isolated places along roads widely spaced homes have such service. At each location the presence of a phone is marked by a sign on the house to insure its potential use when necessary.

In general the Middle Fringe Zone's people are 10-24 hours by land transport from the Continuous Settlement Region. Though air service may shorten this from two places one generally proceeds into or out of the zone by land routes which are rather indirect. At the southern edge of the zone the change to the Inner Fringe Zone is rather abrupt. In part it has been so for many years because of its acceptance as a southern limit of primarily underdeveloped Finland. This reflects a series of sensed differences in Finnish ways of living but it is clearly observable geographically in the distribution of permanent residences (Fig. 7), railroads (Fig. 8), and roads (Fig. 9).

NOTES TO CHAPTER 2

1. Data on basic population and numbers are included in: Tilastollinen Päätoimisto, *Tilastotiedotus,* Vä 1970: 2, Helsinki, 30.1.1970, mimeo. (annual population figures 1890-1967 incl.),; The Geographical Society of Finland, *Suomi, A General Handbook on the Geography of Finland,* Helsinki, 1952; R. R. Platt (ed.), *Finland and Its Geography,* New York, 1955; A. Sømme (ed.), *A Geography of Norden,* Oslo, 1960; The Geographical Society of Finland, *Atlas of Finland, 1960,* Helsinki, 1961.

2. The Geographical Society of Finland, *Suomi, ..., op. cit.,* pp. 381-400.

3. Tilastollinen Päätoimisto, *op. cit.,* Vä 1970: 1 and The Nordic Council, *Yearbook of Nordic Statistics, 1970,* Stockholm, 1971, p. 24.

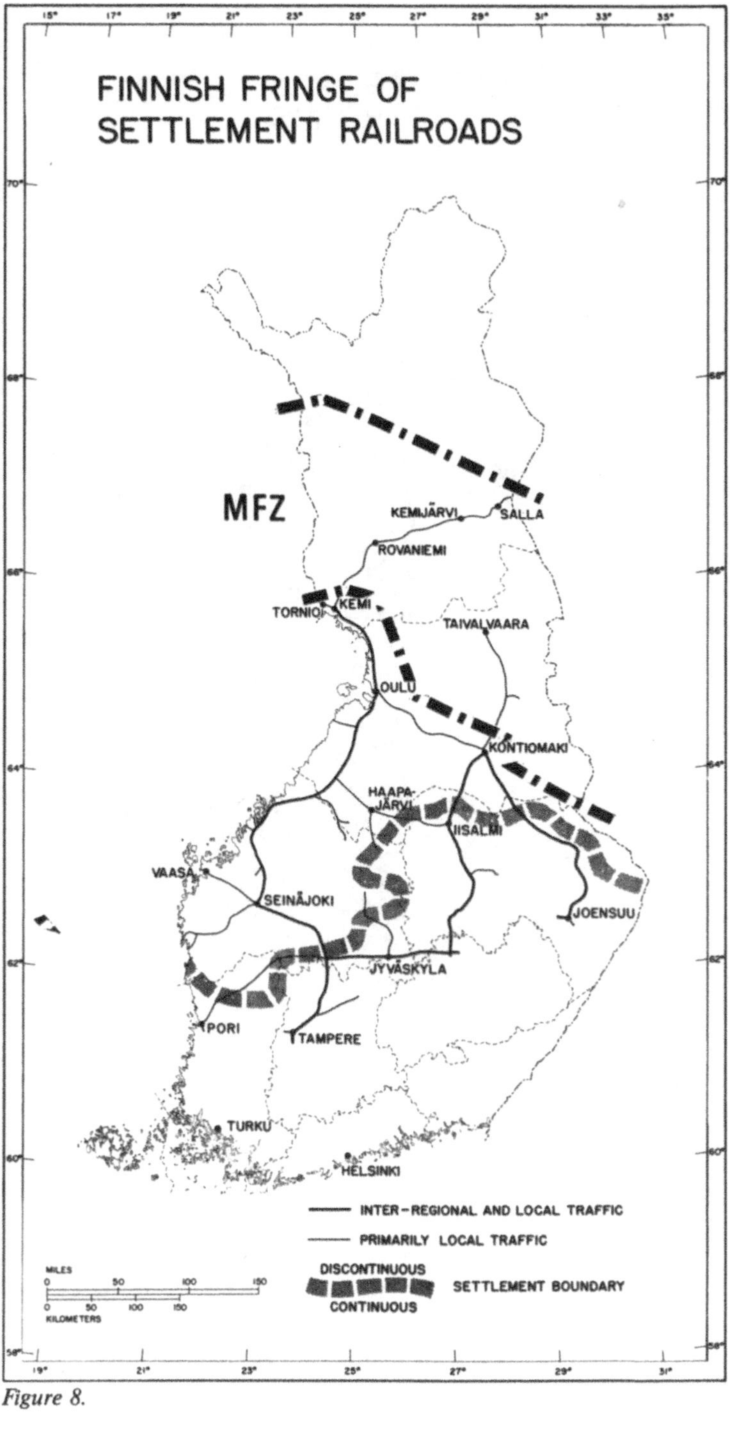
FINNISH FRINGE OF
SETTLEMENT RAILROADS
MFZ
KEMIJÄRVI
SALLA
ROVANIEMI
TORNIO
KEMI
TAIVALVAARA
OULU
KONTIOMAKI
HAAPA-
JÄRVI
IISALMI
VAASA
SEINÄJOKI
JOENSUU
JYVÄSKYLA
PORI
TAMPERE
TURKU
HELSINKI
INTER-REGIONAL AND LOCAL TRAFFIC
PRIMARILY LOCAL TRAFFIC
DISCONTINUOUS
SETTLEMENT BOUNDARY
CONTINUOUS
MILES
KILOMETERS

Figure 8.

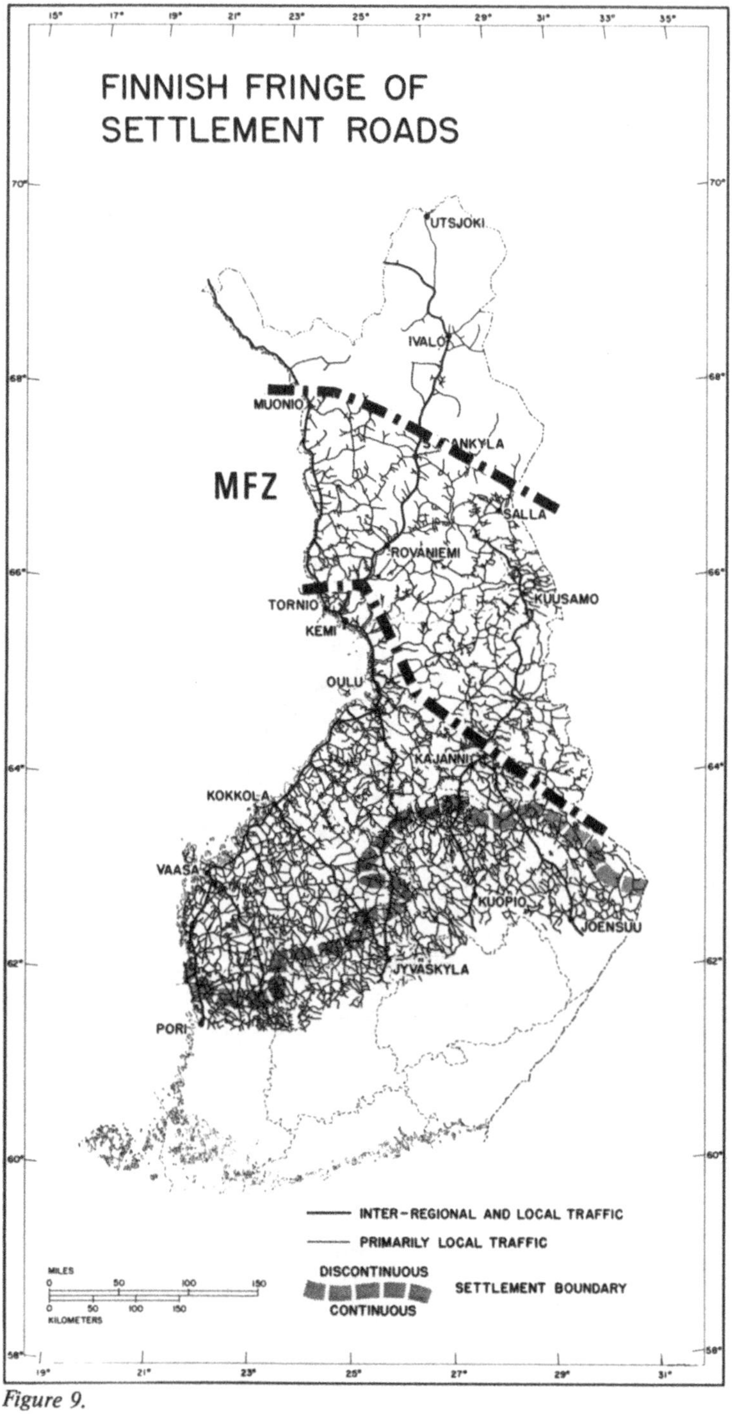
FINNISH FRINGE OF
SETTLEMENT ROADS
UTSJOKI
IVALO
MUONIO
SODANKYLA
MFZ
SALLA
ROVANIEMI
KUUSAMO
TORNIO
KEMI
OULU
KAJAANI
KOKKOLA
VAASA
KUOPIO
JOENSUU
JYVÄSKYLA
PORI
INTER-REGIONAL AND LOCAL TRAFFIC
PRIMARILY LOCAL TRAFFIC
DISCONTINUOUS
CONTINUOUS
SETTLEMENT BOUNDARY
MILES
0 50 100 150
0 50 100 150
KILOMETERS

Figure 9.

4. A. Majava, Migrations Between Finland and Sweden since 1945, in The Scandinavian Demographic Society, *The Second Scandinavian Demographic Symposium,* Stockholm, 1970, pp. 111-118; A. Majava, *Väestönmuutokset Talousalueittain ja Kunnittain Vuosina 1951-1966,* Valtakunnansuunnittelutoimiston Julkaisusarja A:21, Helsinki, 1968 (English summary pp. 91-94).

5. A. Majava, Population Trends in Finland since 1950, *Yearbook of Population Research in Finland,* XI, Helsinki, 1969, pp. 91-100, ref. on p. 94.

6. K. Rikkinen, Markov Chain Analysis of Inter-Provincial Migration in Finland, *Fennia,* v. 108, 1971, pp. 5-19 and T. Hartman, *Kunnittainen Väestöemmuste Vuoteen 2000 Saakka,* I & II, Helsinki, 1969.

7. H. Smeds, Finland, in A. Sømme, *op. cit.,* p. 160.

8. K. Hakulinen, Alueellisia laskelmia Suomen väestöstä 1910-1960, *Terra,* v. 80, 1968, pp. 128-141, ref. on p. 129.

9. The Geographical Society of Finland, *Suomi .....,* pp. 381-400; R. R. Platt (ed.) *op. cit.,* pp. 130-135; W. R. Mead, *op. cit.,* pp. 183-204; The Geographical Society of Finland, *Suomen Kartasto,* 1960, *op. cit.,* plate 14; Colonisation Department, Ministry of Agriculture, *Colonisation Activity in Finland Before and After the World War II,* Helsinki, c1952, mimeo.; A. Løddesøl, Hurtigkolonisasjonen i Finland, *Ny Jord,* 1941, pp. 1-32; W. R. Mead, The Cold Farm in Finland, Resettlement of Finland's Displaced Farmers, *Geographical Review,* v. 41, 1951, pp. 529-543; K. U. Pihkala, Die Neusiedlung in den Waldgebieten Finnlands, *Innere Kolonisation,* v. 14, 1965, pp. 173-176; H. Smeds, Post War Land Clearance and Pioneering Activities in Finland, *Fennia,* v. 83, 1960, pp. 1-31; V. Vennamo and O. Jaakkola, *Finland and Its Internal Resettlement Activity,* Helsinki, c1956, mimeo.; V. Vennamo, *Some Aspects of Post-War Settlement Activity and Reconstruction Work in Finland and the Principles Adopted,* Helsinki, 1959, mimeo.; H. Waris and J. Siipi, *Resettlement of Displaced Persons in Finland,* Helsinki, 1952, mimeo.; M. Palomäki, Post War Pioneering in Finland, *Fennia,* v. 84, 1959, pp. 1-23; and H. Smeds, Recent Changes in the Agricultural Geography of Finland, *Fennia,* v. 87, 1962, pp. 1-19.

10. A. Majava, *Väestön.....,* *op. cit.,* pp. 91-92; G. Beyer, *Rural Migrants in Urban Setting,* The Hague, 1963, pp. 141-152.

11. K. Hakulinen, *op. cit.,* p. 138 (Fig. 13).

12. Valtakunnansuunnittelutoimiston, *Väestön Levinneisyys Suomessa, 1967,* No. A:22, Helsinki, 1968, 48 pp. and 4 maps, scale 1/400,000; these maps also have been combined into a single map, scale of 1/1,000,000, which was published separately.

13. The Geographical Society of Finland, *Atlas.....,* *op. cit.,* plates 16 and 17 and H. Smeds, The Distribution of Urban and Rural Population in Southern Finland, 1950, *Fennia,* v. 81, 1957, pp. 1-21 and map, scale 1/400,000.

14. Valtakunnan....., *op. cit.,* Map IV, scale 1/400,000 and Map 1, scale 1/1,000,000.

15. K. H. Stone, The Concepts of Isolation, *Geoforum,* 11, 1972, pp. 74-77.

16. K. H. Stone, Finnish Fringe of Settlement Zones, *Tijdschrift voor Economische en Sociale Geografie,* v. 57, 1966, pp. 222-232, ref. on pp. 223 and 226.

17. S. Jaatinen, Expansion and Retreat of Settlement in the Southwestern Archipelago of Finland, *Fennia,* v. 84, 1960, Part I, pp. 39-65 and S. Jaatinen, *Atlas över Skargårds-Finland,* Helsingfors, 1960, Plate 15.

18. K. H. Stone, Finnish....., *op. cit.,* pp. 226, 227, and 230.

Chapter 3

ELEMENTS OF THE FINNISH PROCESS OF COLONIZING

First of the modern populating currents in Lapland was the colonizing. Initiated by necessities imposed by the treaties, it was continued into the 1960s by various governmental supports. Within Lapland Province alone 61 major colonies were formed to include more than 1500 families. By this action Finland became one of the world's more experienced nations in the recent planning and executing of new rural settling. The analyses of the forces exerted in administering, selecting settlers, determining the form of a colony, timing the various actions, and financing provide, therefore, one of the few records available that may be used elsewhere in a growing ecumene. It was, in fact, this potential use for planning in other parts of the world which prompted the start of this study in 1955 for it was clear by then that new rural settling is a normal and continuing action in the world but one which has been too little studied for development of international guides. Much more data remain to be obtained for analysis beyond this start.

Administration

It must be recognized from the first that new settling in Finland, like that in any nation, has taken place because the government wished it. Either national laws foster new settling or a national administration permits it. Finnish new settling has been related to the economic need for more production of wood and milk products, to a national zeal to expand the occupied area, to a possible military desire of a "buffer zone" along the eastern border, and to the political wishes of a party in power. It is not confounding, then, that Finnish officials in responsible positions have had varying attitudes about the advisability of encouraging new rural settling in northern Finland. But such was initially forced on the Finns. And it went on. With such an initiation, one can hardly expect to justify the actions entirely on economic bases. Still, generally effective direction was given.

Administration of the settling is from national to local levels. The principal agency (*Asutushallitus,* Fin.) is headquartered in Helsinki and is the center for final approval of action. Next are the 26 regional commissions (*Jordispositionkommissioner,* Swed.) which do the planning for colonization under the Land Utilization Act of 1959. In Lapland there are six such commissions. Each is composed, as in Rovaniemi, of a surveyor, an agronomist, and a forester. These are permanent members and to them are added, at the level of the commune (the minor civil division), technicians and two of the area's settlers to act on local matters. These boards' principal tasks are to plan for new settling and to improve the economic bases of existing farms.

The commissions administer in general by way of the state's colonization laws. These are varied and numerous. However, most of the settling since 1936 has been governed by one of four laws. The first, Law 110, was passed in 1936 so it was not designed to meet an emergency and it did not provide subsidy for creating a new, or "cold", farm in a previously uncleared area; however, some payments were made later to settlers under this law.

A second decree, the Land Acquisition Act of 5 May 1945, was the one under which most new settling took place. It defined principles under which land could be required for settlement, provided for governmental authority to expropriate, and indicated how grants of land and Finnish Marks (FMK) would be made. Important specifications were: a maximum of 630,000 FMK[1] in premiums for a "cold farm", 756,000 FMK in premiums for DPs and war widows, 5 per cent additional allowances for each child if there were more than three in a family, and a requirement to erect buildings and clear about 10 hectares (25 acres) on each farm. Those covered by the act, in addition to the DPs and widows, were former soldiers, war invalids, and war orphans.

In 1958 Law 6 was passed. This took the place of all prior colonization acts by combining most of their elements into one regulation. Then, a year later, by the Land Use Act of 1959, the most recent legislation encouraging new rural settling was passed to increase the subsidies. Building premiums were raised to 1,200,000 FMK and clearing premiums to 72,000 FMK per hectare while the allowance for children was the same for more than two, rather than three, per family. By then, though, as is noted in Chapter 4, starting colonies was nearly over and the new act applied, and applies, to those settlers completing the plans for colonization. So it was the 1945 Act on which most of Lapland's contemporary immigration was founded.

The commissions also draw up the contracts with individual settlers. Each agreement is divisible into two periods of time: the first five years and the next 31 years. During the first period the state retains ownership and the settlers have to perform certain tasks, described below. If these are done satisfactorily the farm can then be bought and the settler either has 31 years to pay the sum agreed upon or he may contract to purchase the place after 13 years on the property.

The critical nature of the first five years is readily apparent. During it the state grants most of its premiums (subsidies). And in that period the local board can note the qualities of a settler by his accomplishments according to the five-year plan. An example of this plan might be:

First year :	Build sauna and dig well, acquire materials for construction of residence, clear area for residence, and clear .5 hectare (1 1/4 acres) of land for cropping.
Second year:	Build residence so it can be used for protection against rain or snow and clear another .5 hectare of land for cropping.
Third year :	Complete residence, acquire materials for construction of barn, and clear another .5 hectare of land.
Fourth year:	Do principal construction work on barn and clear another .5 hectare of land.
Fifth year :	Complete the barn and clear another .5 hectare of land.

Although this period proved to be too short in many instances, it provided a testing period during which the intentions of the settlers' uses of state funds could be measured by the local boards with a fairly high degree of accuracy. Furthermore, numerous settlers completed these requirements in only three years. In general appearance of farmsteads, though, the procedure leads to a common early scene in which buildings are emphasized and clearings are not (Fig. 10). However, it must be remembered that forestry is combined with agriculture in Finland and that work in a settler's woods is planned for as a major source of income in this first period; such activity may not be seen easily.

Original recommendations for the creation of a colony come from one of three possible sources: 1) a colonization supervisor (of which there are 20 in Finland), 2) a regional commission, and 3) a local board. When approved the regional commission obtains the land. This has been mostly in state-owned areas but privately-owned parcels have been bought where needed and selection depended on the land's location and physical qualities. The latter are known usually as a result of prior mapping by two societies, one concerned with swamps and the other with mineral soils. Soils, drainage, vegetation, and surface configuration are mapped by university students representing the societies; particular attention is given to the moisture present and to the qualities of the soil and forest.[2] Of course, local officials are familiar with the areas selected and more detailed surveys are often necessary for the specific planning. In general, then, physical qualities have been studied carefully, but geographic situations seem to have attracted less attention.

One administrative principle has been very significant. The general Finnish policy has been to provide much, but definitely not all, of the needs for new settling. Particularly in the earliest phases and with respect to costs. The government has recognized that initial expenditures of funds, effort, and time are often excessive; it has lightened the load by pre-colonization inventories and construction and by subsidies of several types. On the other hand, it has realized that permanence is attained more readily by the settler investing as much of his resources as possible. It appears that the principle has been applied rather well.

Selection of Settlers

Selection of the settlers in Finland depends initially upon their applying. The primary qualifications hinge upon the specific law under which application is made but a consideration of major importance is that applicants be local residents. This means that movements to new colonies have been short distances, perhaps maxima of 30-40 km. (19-25 mi.). The advantages of this are clear: the settlers are familiar with the area, the applicants usually are known by the local boards, and settlers are likely to know each other or be related.

In general, the families selected were large. To Finnish sociologists the northern part of their country has been known as a "very fertile area!" because four of five children per colony family is common. The range is more than double this and some colonists have 11-13 children.[3] It is these numbers that drew the criticism of some officials in the early 1960s; they bemoaned the costs of education but, most of all, they worried about the future when there might be too much population pressure on the forests and land. It was also argued that the great responsibility of a large family when initiating settling put too much strain on the parents. What a suitable size is depends, of course, on the age and sex composition, the health and psychological make-up, the experience, and the economic resources of a family in relation to the proposed occupation. Local boards have tried to take these into account.

Throughout the world the selection of settlers is the "Achilles heel" of new rural settling. Probably less is known about this than any other element in planning of this type. Little has been written on it.[4] In Lapland's colonizing settler selection did not become a problem for several reasons. The short-distance movement to familiar territory eliminated some usual migrational strains. The patriotism of the immigrants prompted additional personal discipline to overcome disappointments and delays. Finnish *sisu* is a further inner strength to resist discomfort. Thus, the selection of settlers for colonizing Lapland was done under unusual conditions which actually contributed more to easing local commissions' problems rather than increasing them. Still, if professional psychological and sociological analyses could be made of the original settlers still in Lapland Province it is probable that much could be learned of value to planners elsewhere.

Geographical Form

A colony's design is the work of its local board. The major effort goes into five elements: roads, drainage lines, farm layout, residential sites, and the designation of common forest and pasture, if any. With respect to roads Finnish planners generally agree it is desirable to center a colony on an existing road so as to be able to start colonizing at the most opportune time as well as to have the possibility of service by a mobile store (which is permitted to start selling at one kilometer (0.6 mi.) from an existing store). Also, it has been felt expedient to have internal circulation by through roads rather than "dead ends". This is more efficient with respect to upkeep (e.g., snow removal) and daily use (e.g., pickup of school children and milk). That the desirable is not always attained is demonstrated by many dead-ends roads in existing colonies (Fig. 10). In general, the main roads are built by the state and the internal routes of a colony by local agencies. Every settler, however, is responsible for the construction of the last 50 meters (164 feet) of the individual access routes.

Artificial drainage is essential because all colonies are selected

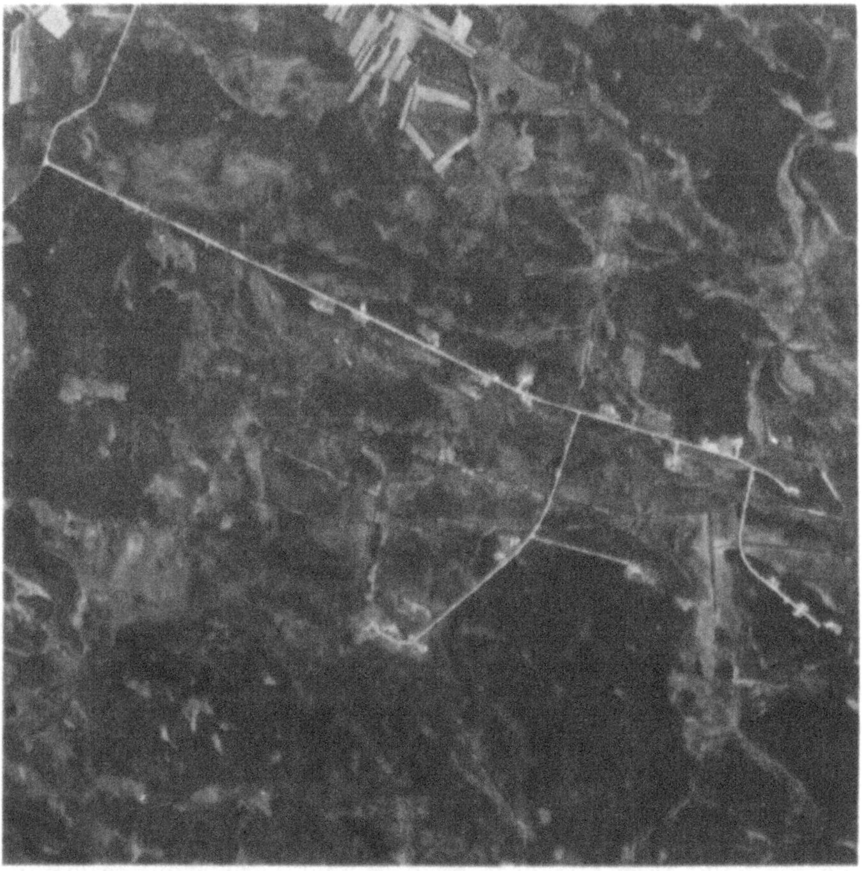

Figure 10. Urriaavan Colony, overview. (See p. 93).

to combine swamp and morainic land, the former for hay and the latter for vegetables and grains. The primary ditches are planned and constructed by the state according to a regional drainage system. The secondary and local ditches are tied into this plan by a local drainage engineer but the work on and cost of construction of individual farms' drains are dependent upon the settlers involved.

A Finnish colony may include three types of ownership parcels. There are farms, small farms, and homesites. The recent colonies have been predominantly farms but a few included homesites (Chapter 4). Considering farms their sizes vary. In the sample colonies discussed below the mean area is 55-275 hectares (136-679 acres) with most being about 200 hectares (494 acres); however, many are larger as the ranges in size are 90-370 hectares (222-914 acres). These include about 25-30 hectares (62-74 acres) of arable land and roughly 128-154 hectares (308-370 acres) of forest. The sizable ranges reflect the variations in type and quality of swamp and forest. Local boards laid out farms so as to distribute various kinds of land somewhat equally, so variation in size of farms may be anticipated. Further, a separation of a farm's fields is the usual case and many farms are composed of five to seven separate pieces each, most of which are within five to 10 km. (three to six mi.) of the farmstead.

Residences are seldom sited where planners consider them to be most efficiently located. Preferred sites are road junctions or close spacings along a central road so that stops for pickups (e.g., students, milk) could be concentrated. The settlers' choices, however, have been the more expensive scattered locations. This has a parallel in Alaska's Matanuska Valley, where colonists quickly moved homes that were originally clustered at road junctions.[5] Apparently rural settlers can be too close to each other as well as too far apart. More specifically, though, Finnish planners have learned to leave sufficient space next to lakes in colonies that adjoin them. Settlers prefer to have their dwellings on the lake side of the road for access to the water but homes need to be above the level at which freezing air "collects" over the lake; potato fields at lake edges are subject to the earliest frosts. Therefore, roads need to be placed far enough from the lakes for a compromise location to be attained.

Timing of Actions

The timing of the various settling activities is crucial. It requires much more study but some guides are clear from desirable and undesirable results in northern Finland.

Main drainage ditches need to be dug at least two years prior to colonizing. This is to allow water table adjustment and to make other work easier. Also, main and secondary roads are needed by the time of colonizing; Finnish settlers are expected to cut timber for income in the first years, so roads (probably all-weather) are necessary to move that product out as well as equipment and materials in. Without early ditching and roads a considerable delay of all settling and building is likely; it must be remembered that a three-month holdup at a critical time in an early year of settling may force an additional wait of up to nine months more. Several of these features are reflected by the 6-45 month delays in the sample colonies (Table 3, Chapter 4) but there were, to be sure, personal reasons for some of these.

The construction of buildings in the sample colonies shows the significance of timing. At 58% of the farms the sauna was the first building completed, its mean construction time was 6-10 months.

Quite often the sauna served as a temporary dwelling until the residence could be built (Fig. 11). The house not only took longer

Figure 11. Puupuolivarvikkon Colony, farmstead. (See p. 93).

to construct but also required more money so its construction was put off in most of the contract plans until the second or third year. The large size of the families, however, and the fact that the whole family usually moved to the Finnish farm right at the start (and had much "togetherness" in the small sauna during at least the first winter!) encouraged completion of the residence as soon as possible.

When barns were constructed was also important. Most of the sample colony families needed milk regularly when they went to the farms so one or two cows were taken along. For them a temporary barn had to be built and was satisfactory for two or three years. Not only was milk obtained for the family but cream was available for sale in the second or third year to supplement the income from the forests. This money provided some of that needed to develop a herd whose milk could be sold regularly by the fifth year. This sequence of events was anticipated by the local boards and was, in fact, encouraged. It appears to have served several of the settlers' needs quite well.

As noted earlier, the first five years is deemed critical. That time must be used very efficiently to promote continuation of the settling and to delay discouragement. There is much to do. And much money to be spent. Assuming that main roads and drainage ditches are operational when settling begins, an individual settler has a number of things to accomplish nearly at once. An access road to the farmstead site is essential, even if the settler only has a horse or motor bike; equipment for clearing must get in and out and trucks must be able to deliver construction materials and take out timber and farm products. Water is essential; that which is potable for the family as well as amounts needed for animals and construction (e.g., to make cement) and all of these the year around. Usually this requires the digging of a well. The family and animals must be housed, if only temporarily. Secondary ditching of the swamps must be undertaken to create crop land. The residential site, usually on wooded morainic land (Fig. 10), needs to be cleared. Woods roads have to be established and time spent at woods work to provide funds. Materials for construction and farming must acquired. And, if they can be afforded, lines for electricity and telephone need to be allowed for but usually these are postponed in older north Finnish colonies. It is clear that many hours of hard work per day are essential in the first year. And all this is further complicated by the climatic characteristics of being dry in the first six weeks of the summer and then becoming progressively wetter in the next six weeks. Thus, timing in this first year is absolutely crucial.

The next four years are similar. Priorities have to be set with respect to individual families' needs to provide money, shelter, food, and other necessities while developing greater degrees of permanence in all of them. So permanent buildings must be constructed, more land cleared for cropping, herds built up, and provisions made for continued shopping and expanded marketing.

Meanwhile community facilities are another necessity. Schools must be built and manned if none is not already near enough. If stores are not present arrangements are necessary for traveling stores (especially equipped buses with perishable and dry goods) to be present periodically. Milk pick-up platforms and schedules need to be set up. Recreational and religious facilities are advisable. Nor is all the hard work over in these first five years, they are only the initial critical period. Clearly it is a time when settlers and officials can use all the cooperation and aid that is possible for if proper coordination of activities is not ensured the provision alone is not enough.

Costs

Total costs of Finnish colonization are difficult to assess. Such is often the case for many social and personal costs are not available, some charges are based on artificial figures, accounting methods change, money values vary, and prices of items and services needed or sold fluctuate greatly in post-war periods. Still, selected costs are useful as general indicators.

The settling program was designed as a means of maintaining individual pride and initiative while developing the country according to national desires. In keeping with these objectives the state paid 20-25% of the total cost of a new farm and loaned the settlers as much as 50% of the rest. Repayment on the loans has been at 5% annually, three of which was interest. At the judgment of local boards, settlers have been permitted to postpone annual payments without losing their farms.

Costs of the land were based on 1944 valuations. Rough average prices for the buildings were 1,500,000 Finnish Marks (FMK) for a house, 1,000,000 FMK for a barn, and 250,000-300,000 FMK for a sauna and loans on these were 50-60% of the costs. In addition, the settler was charged from 5-10% of the total expense for building roads and drainage ditches. In northern Finland the main ditches cost in the early 1960s about 500 FMK per meter or 30,000 FMK per hectare while the average road costs were 3,000,000-4,000,000 FMK per kilometer of main routes and 1,000,000 FMK per kilometer of other types. Other direct charges to settlers were for clearing; to clear mineral soils during the early 1960s cost as much as 200,000 FMK per hectare and of swamp land 100,000-150,000 FMK per hectare. This expense varied, of course, with the amount of work done by a settler's family.

The aid in premiums differed with the circumstances of the individual settlers, the laws under which they settled, their non-farm income, and their initiative. As noted above, under the Land Acquisition Act of 5 May 1945 a maximum of 630,000 FMK was allowed for a "cold farm" while DPs and war widows got as much as 756,000 FMK. These sums were granted if the settlers constructed buildings and cleared about 10 hectares (25 acres) of land. But, if they had three or more children when the contract was drawn up they received 5% off the total price for each child and any child born thereafter. Under the more recent act the cold farm premium increased to 1,200,000 FMK, the clearing premium to 72,000 FMK per hectare, and the children clause reduced to two.

By an earlier system the subsidies for cultivating (or clearing) arable land were on a sliding scale. For up to five hectares (12 acres) of cleared land the farmer received 63,000 FMK each, for between 5 and 10 (12-25 acres) it was 56,000, for between 10 and 15 (25-37 acres) it was 49,000, for between 15 and 25 (37-62 acres) it was 42,000, and for more than 25 hectares (62 acres) cleared no aid was provided. Thus, the kinds of direct help given these settlers varied with several conditions.

To be sure, there have been indirect subsidies as well. These new farms were based on the production of milk and forest products. But the milk price had to be subsidized greatly. In part this was due to the distance from Helsinki and in part to the inefficiency, at least at first, of milk production. By the third year of settling, most farmers had cream to sell two or three times a week and by the fifth year many had milk ready for daily pickup. But the small amounts, the number of stops, and the long hauls to local creameries put a strain on Valio, Finland's largest cooperative, not only to keep up the incoming flow of milk, but also the export of its products, even though high quality has been maintained. In the 1960s it was estimated that without the subsidy northern Finland's milk production probably would collapse; the field-reservation program of 1969 substantiated this more in northern Finland than elsewhere but its principle effect was social.[6]

Another form of subsidization has been the winter work program. Because of the fairly widespread unemployment in winter, the state has granted much money for work to be conducted only in that season. Though the transportation of some materials is easier at that time some of the other activities cost more. For example, the digging of drainage ditches in winter has cost from two and a half to three times more than in summer and some of the work on roads has been even more expensive. One may admit that economical construction is not the only value in the area, but indirect subsidies such as these make evaluation of the total costs of settling somewhat ineffective.

An additional price for colonizing has been paid. This is a yet unmeasured societal charge. Seldom is it even referred to in planning for new settling but Johnson called it "the social costs".[7] This alludes to how much more expensive it is to have people with higher and higher degrees of local and regional isolation and it is related to the inconveniences to these individuals as a result of isolations. In northern Finland these societal charges may be quite high but, as in other countries where new rural settling has been undertaken in a Region of Discontinuous Settlement, the expense has been absorbed as a total national item and its specifics overlooked. Surely it is more expensive to have singles and clusters of rural dwellings[8] and long distances of roads with no homes along them than the costs of roads and services provided in a Region of Continuous Settlement. But Finland wanted new settling in its north so it had to pay this charge. Just as surely, the new north Finnish settlers were inconvenienced, at least in the initial phases of settling. They had to go without materials or services when needed or pay more for them than in the south. Still, many disregarded these costs in time, convenience, and money because, if displaced persons, they preferred the freedom of Finland or, if not displaced, they considered it an advantage to live on a farm of their own.

NOTES TO CHAPTER 3

1. In the late 1950s an average exchange rate was about 320 FMK per U.S.A. dollar or about \$3125 U.S.A. per 1,000,000 FMK. However, this rate does not permit direct comparisons of cost between the two countries because of: 1) differences in prices for the same items in the two nations, 2) a relatively recent change in the valuation of Finnish Marks to roughly 4 FMK/ \$1 U.S.A.; and 3) the 19 December 1971 devaluation of the dollar so that the new central exchange rate became 4.10 FMK/ \$1 U.S.A., around which daily quotations may move freely up to 2.25% in either direction. For these reasons equivalents in U.S.A. dollars are omitted in the text so that only relative costs of settling activities in Finland are noted.

2. Copies of the originals of these maps, at scales of 1/50,000 to 1/8,000, are available at cost from the governmental archives in Rovaniemi.

3. One can hardly give much credence to some Finnish reports that families are large in northern Finland because of the allowances for children in the 1945 and 1959 Acts. The proof of family size throughout the world remains largely to be discovered and none of the suppositions about the uniqueness of Lapland families is based on scientific analysis.

4. H. Meliczek, Selection of Settlers for Land Settlement Schemes, *Land Reform,* No. 1, 1969, pp. 42-55; J. Moris, The Evaluation of Settlement Schemes Performance: A Sociological Appraisal in R. J. Apthorpe (ed.), *Land Settlement and Rural Development in Eastern Africa,* Kampala, 1968, pp. 79-102; K. Z. Raschig, Menschen in Neuen Siedlungen, *Hauswirtschaft und Wissenschaft,* v. 14, 1966, pp. 45-51; E. Kramer, *On Selection of Settlers,* U.S. Dept. of Agriculture (?), Washington (?), 1935 (?).

5. K. H. Stone, *Alaskan Group Settlement: The Matanuska Valley Colony,* U.S. Department of the Interior, Washington, 1950. The reverse situation, however, applies in Norway where colonists' dwellings are located exactly by officials in Oslo and the subsidies are granted only if these locations are used.

6. S. Jaatinen and U. Kärkkäinen, *Vuoden 1969 Pellonvaraustoiminta,* Helsingin Yliopiston Maantieteen Laitoksen Julkaisuja, Sarja B, No. 7, Helsinki, 1971.

7. H. A. Johnson, *The Social Costs of Isolated Settlement,* (paper presented at Sixth Alaska Science Congress, June 1955), Palmer, Alaska, 1955, pp. 1-5, mimeo.

8. These terms are defined in K. H. Stone, Multiple-Scale Classifications for Rural Settlement Geography, *Acta Geographica* (Helsinki), v. 20, 1968, pp. 307-328, particularly pp. 311-317.

Chapter 4

NORTHERN FINNISH POST-WAR COLONIZING

Between 1946 and 1967 some 61 major colonization districts were established and occupied in Lapland Province. Each has such general unity that it may be termed a colony. Specifically, though, the colonies vary in degrees of isolation, date of settling, type of settlers, size, and speed of settling. To illustrate these differences five sample colonies were selected for more detailed study between 1956 and 1970.

Even more important the sample colonies show strong similarities. Some of these are results of national policies and trends discussed in Chapters 2 and 3; others are the products of certain families settling on specific farms at definite times. In total all this settling produced significant changes in the geography of Lapland's rural settlement. In the colonies alone 1528 families were planned for and nearly all are there. This approximately 7500 people, mostly on farms, and perhaps half as many more on scattered single farms reflected a superior national governmental effort. The desire was to provide homes for its displaced citizens, to increase economic opportunities for its people, to produce more, and, possibly, to create a more densely settled zone next to the Soviet border as well as to garner votes for local politicians. It did all of these. In sum there was created one of the world's primary examples of expansion of its inhabited area on a regional scale.

The Lapland Colonies in General

Geographically the 61 colonies are in the southern part of the province (Table 2). This is the Middle Fringe of Settlement Zone where there are moderate to low degrees of regional isolation as well as similar grades of local isolation, described above in Chapter 2. Within the MFZ the colonies are scattered throughout with two exceptions. First is that they were usually placed within or at the edge of already occupied land (Fig. 2) albeit a low density of settlement; few were sited in totally uninhabited areas. Secondly, there

Table 2. Major New Rural Colonies in Lapland Province, Finland, 1946-1967

Commune	General Provincial Location	Colony	Year Begun	Planned No. of Family Units Total	Agri.	Homesite	No. of Displ. Pop. Families	Area (Hectares) Total	State	Private
Alatornio	SW	Aapajärven	1950	36	31	5	7	4024	1131	2893
		Lautamaan	1948	28	0	28	0	884	0	884
		Susiaavan	1950	12	12	0	3	2483	1131	1352
Inari	NE	Nanguniemen	1952	13	0	13	8	2088	2088	0
		Pikku-Petsamon	1948	10	1	9	7	758	758	0
		Sikovuonon	1952	8	0	8	7	1182	1182	0
Kemijärvi	SC	Autiosaaren	1948	10	7	3	0	802	0	802
		Kalkiaisen	1946	23	19	4	0	3810	3585	225
		Luokka-aavan	1951	17	9	8	3	1922	1360	562
		Morkkaperän	1946	12	12	0	0	2869	2618	251
		Päiväjoen	1948	13	13	0	0	1796	1342	454
		Vuostimon	1947	19	19	0	0	2419	2417	2
Kittilä	NC	Kuusanjoen	1946	9	8	1	0	1603	0	1603
		Liinajavuoman	1946	8	4	4	0	1005	0	1005
		Naakenavuoman	1946	13	9	4	0	1803	0	1803
		Sirkan	1951	6	6	0	1	886	886	0
		Veitti ja Ratasvuoman	1947	13	13	0	0	1593	0	1593
Kolari	WC	Pasmajärven	1946	15	14	1	0	2626	0	2626
Muonio	WC	Kaalamanniemen	1964	25	25	0	0			
Pelkosenniemi	EC	Aapajärven	1946	40	20	20	0	2676	2676	0
		Härkäjoen	1949	5	5	0	0	1077	1077	0
		Saukkoaavan	1949	15	15	0	0	2320	2320	0
Pello	WC	Koutuksen	1951	27	24	3	0	4847	3849	998
		Naamijoen	1949	30	18	12	0	4778	3807	971
Ranua	SC	Kelan	1947	6	2	4	0	676	676	0
		Ruonan	1946	10	6	4	1	1390	872	518
		Toljan	1950	12	12	0	0	2216	2216	0
Rovaniemi	SC	Haukijärvi-Taipole	1967	50	50	0	0			
		Koiramännikön	1949	8	5	3	0	916	916	0
		Louejoen	1950	18	18	0	0	3845	3704	141
		Välijoen	1951	61	49	12	6	10707	10707	0
Salla	SE	Ahma-aavan	1952	7	7	0	0	2621	2621	0
		Ahvenselän	1948	37	33	4	37	5087	5087	0

Commune	General Provincial Location	Colony	Year Begun	Planned No. of Family Units Total	Agri.	Homesite	No. of Displ. Pop. Families	Area (Hectares) Total	State	Private
		Haisujängän	1953	18	18	0	0	4094	4089	5
		Hossoaavan	1955	14	14	0	0	2953	2953	0
		Isoaavan	1955	18	18	0	0	2675	0	2675
		Kouteloaapa	1958	30	30	0	0	5744		
		Kurijoen	1950	86	71	15	86	12066	12066	0
		Lapajärven	1950	16	15	1	16	1661	1661	0
		Maaselän	1952	15	15	0	0	4624	2808	1816
		Naruskan	1946	27	19	8	27	2121	2121	0
		Oulangen	1950	51	35	16	51	5717	5717	0
		Pahkakummun	1948	66	51	15	66	7408	7408	0
		Puupuolivarvikon	1948	86	66	20	86	8504	8504	0
		Tuohiaavan	1946	35	27	8	62	4379	4379	0
		Urriaavan	1955	18	18	0	0	3987	3983	4
		Vallovaaran	1948	101	75	26	101	10325	10325	0
Savukoski	EC	Matka-aavan	1950	12	7	5	0	1053	1053	0
		Niemijoen	1949	7	5	2	0	847	847	0
		Poristeen	1947	8	7	1	0	1043	1043	0
Sodankylä	NC	Emauksen	1945	20	4	16	0	892	665	227
		Lisma-aavan	1953	40	40	0	2	8504	8504	0
		Kursanmännikon	1948	4	4	0	1	764	764	0
Tervola	SW	Kätkävaaran	1950	54	54	0	6	6595	5917	678
		Sivakkajoen	1952	20	20	0	13	3183	1418	1765
		Varejoen	1948	46	46	0	36	9030	5602	3428
Ylitornio	SW	Kapustavuoman	1952	29	29	0	0	7900	7406	494
		Kuijasjoen	1948	23	23	0	1	5287	4939	348
		Lähejängän	1950	12	12	0	1	2284	2039	245
		Ratasvuoman	1949	40	24	16	0	4199	3098	1101
		Väystäjän	1950	16	16	0	1	3121	2721	400
Totals				1528	1229	299	636	208669*	**	**

*Excluding two newest colonies.

**Incomplete

Source: Data from files and maps of Ministry of Colonization, Lapland Office, Rovaniemi, 1960 and 1970.

are three departures from evenness of distribution: 1) a concentration is in the southeast, in Salla commune, where there are 16 colonies which include 41% of the provincial total of colonist families (no other commune has as much as 10%) and 82% of Lapland's total of Displaced Persons in colonies; 2) there are no colonies in Posio commune, adjoining Salla on the southwest; and 3) a large part of Rovaniemi commune in the southwest has no colonies (Fig. 2).

Why these locations? Several reasons are known or surmised. The southern part of Lapland is immediately west of and very similar in physical qualities to the Salla-Kuusamo sector whence so many DPs originated. Southern Lapland has less regional isolation and larger areas of lower local isolation than the northern part. Pre-colonization farmers living with 2 1/2 - 5 km. (1 1/2 - 3 mi.) of at least the edge of a colony meant that the new settlers usually had some facilities and experienced nearby neighbors; it saved time and expense and reduced the social isolation. Further, this area was one of large blocks of state-owned land which made planning for large colonies and acquisition easier. Lastly, Finland has long been pushing northward with the hope of making its more distant and thinly-settled provinces more self-sufficient economically.

In date of starting most of the colonies were begun by 1953. The years of greatest activity were the five post-war ones of 1946 through 1950; during them 70% of the colonies were formed and of the 42% (636 families) of the people that were DPs most were colonized in the same period. Thus, until 1950 was a first period of mostly emergency resettling. Then continued new rural settling by others who qualified, especially as war-time soldiers, and new starts took place in only 1955 (3), 1958 (1), 1964 (1), and 1967 when the last colony, Haukijärvi-Taipole, was begun.

In number of families per colony there was considerable range. The planned number averaged 25 of which 20 were on farms and the rest on homesites. But actually they varied from 5 to 101 families per colony and 0 to 75 agricultural units. That most colonizing originated for a farming-forestry combination is shown by 82% of the units being planned as agricultural sites (for dairying and lumbering); 28 of the colonies were totally agricultural sites and 14 more were predominantly so (with less than 5 homesites). Still, there were differences inasmuch as homesite numbers ranged from 0 to 28 and three colonies were composed only of this type of parcel.

In size the colonies also differ greatly. An average size is about 3500 hectares (8649 acres or 13.5 sq. mi.) but the range is from 676 hectares (1670 acres or 2.6 sq. mi.) to 12,066 hectares (29,653 acres or 46.3 sq. mi.). Most of this land, 82%, was state-owned and at least 27 of the colonies were formed entirely of land originally in public ownership (Table 2).

These general differences and similarities in the colonies are readily seen. But it is the similarities in details that are most significant in analyzing the process of new rural settling. To note these specifics five sample colonies were chosen to cut across the ranges in characteristics discussed above. They are, in order of older to newer colonies: Pasmajärven, Välijoen, Kapustavuoman, Lisma-aavan, and Urriaavan (Fig. 2). They are in all directions and between 38 - 176 km. (24 - 109 mi.) by road from Rovaniemi, were started between 1946 and 1955, are from below average in number of families to above average, include similar ranges in farm-size and farm-building characteristics, and reflect similarities and differences in colonists' desires and activities (Table 3). Consideration of the individual colonies makes clear some guides for new rural settling elsewhere in the world.

Pasmajärven Colony

Located at the central western edge of the Lapland MFZ, Pasmajärven Colony has a somewhat unique combination of characteristics.

Figure 12. Pasmajärven Colony, farmstead. (See p. 93).

It represents the older colonies, is a mixture of 16 colony and 14 non-colony settlers of wide-ranging starting dates, has a small number of rather small farms, is fragmented areally, was founded on privately owned land, and has developed slowly.

The slow growth probably reflects several features of the colony. Certainly an important one is its high degrees of isolation. Regionally it is deep in the Middle Fringe Zone about half way between Tornio and Muonio and only 35 km. (22 mi.) from the Swedish border (the Tornio River). Locally isolation is also high because the colony's position 128 km. (79 mi.) NW of Rovaniemi is accessible only indirectly by a two-lane gravel road from the south and northwest which leads to one-lane roads that dead-end within the colonized area. The isolation is emphasized by the area's spotty and shortline pattern of settlement, only one inter-regional road at Sieppijärvi, 24 km. (15 mi.) to the northwest, and a local freight-only railroad 5 km. (3 mi.) farther west.[1] At 67°05′ N. this is hardly enough.

In physical features the colony is somewhat average for northern Finland. All colonists' homes are between 180 and 200 meters (590 and 656 ft.) above sea level on a ground morainic surface ranging from 163 meters (535 ft.) at Pasmajärvi Lake to nearby hilltops averaging 250 meters (820 ft.).[2] This is covered with the usual birch-spruce-pine woods on the drier sites and grass-sedge-moss on the wetter ones (Figs. 12 & 13). The forest may be rated only fair because none of the colonists had woods producing as much as 80 cubic meters per year of, at best, second and third class timber, in comparison with the settlement planners' generally desired 75-125, including higher quality wood.

The colony was started in 1946, during the period of hurried new settling, and was experimental in several respects. One was in the discontinuous nature of the colony's area; it was composed of a major part just north of Aalisjärvi (lake) and four other small sections on northwestward (Fig. 14). In the latter were four pre-colony farms. But in the major part there was a considerable mixing; the range is from non-colonists who settled before the colony to some who came in the late 1960s and colonists who started in 1950 to those who began as recently as 1965 (Table 4).

Sixteen new colony farms were proposed.[3] Most of them are along the single-lane road extending to, and ending at, the southern edge of the colony. The road is in the usual north Finnish position of being uphill from the moraine-swamp junction so that large fields of hay may be placed on drained swamp and small fields of grain and potatoes on the stony mineral soil; it must be remembered that the latter now costs three to four times as much to clear as it does to drain and break swamp soil. All homes but one are on the eastern side of the road though three others were planned to be on the downhill side.

Another cause of slow development may be the relatively small sizes of the farms. The mean is 105 hectares (259 acres) including 21 hectares of arable land and 66 (163 acres) of woods (Table 3). Half of the farms are one-parcel units and the rest have two parcels each but nearly all the colony land has been assigned so expansion of units is dependent upon either local consolidation or use of land elsewhere. Two farms are still undeveloped, even though they have relatively large amounts of arable land, and the problem may be the relative high cost of the farms (Table 4).

Delayed growth was reflected in other ways at Pasmajärven. By 1960

Figure 13. Pasmajärven Colony, fields. (See p. 93).

the mean starting time to construction of buildings was 45 months, nearly double the maximum in the other sample colonies; and the actual constructional periods for houses, barns, and saunas was more than twice as long in the same comparison (Table 3). In fact, in August 1960 the colony hardly appeared viable; no electric power line was present, the nearest telephone was out of the colony at the farm east of the school, the last milk stand was at farm no. 21, two of the houses were unoccupied (farms no. 3 and 5), and two others were

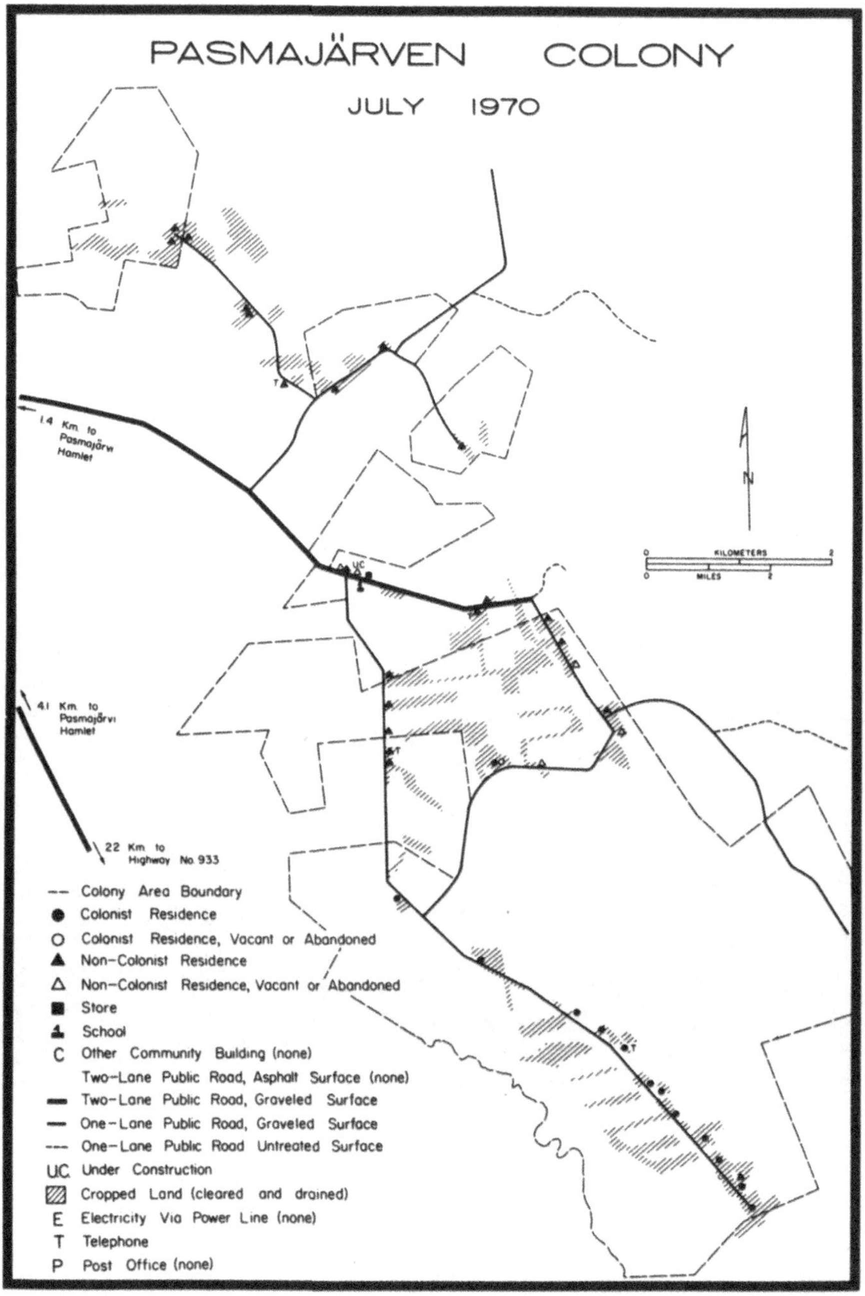
PASMAJÄRVEN COLONY
JULY 1970
1.4 Km. to Pasmajärvi Hamlet
4.1 Km. to Pasmajärvi Hamlet
22 Km. to Highway No. 933
UC
T
N
KILOMETERS
MILES
0
2
Colony Area Boundary
Colonist Residence
Colonist Residence, Vacant or Abandoned
Non-Colonist Residence
Non-Colonist Residence, Vacant or Abandoned
Store
School
C Other Community Building (none)
Two-Lane Public Road, Asphalt Surface (none)
Two-Lane Public Road, Graveled Surface
One-Lane Public Road, Graveled Surface
One-Lane Public Road Untreated Surface
UC Under Construction
Cropped Land (cleared and drained)
E Electricity Via Power Line (none)
T Telephone
P Post Office (none)

Figure 14.

unpainted (though painting was a part of the agreement involving premiums). But some clearing was in evidence at four of the colonists' places and at five of the earlier settlers'. Still several Finnish planners considered the experiment unsuccessful in the early 1960s; as usual this depends upon how success is measured.

Passage of the Land Use Act of 1959 appears to have given the colony new life. Four farms benefitted from the increase in premiums provided by this act in relation to those farms settled under the 1945 act. By 1964 new building construction and new clearings at more than half the farms showed considerable hope. And by then telephones had been installed at farms no. 21 (in the colony) and no. 10 (nearby).

Community service centers have been and are minimal at Pasmajärven Colony. At the northern end of the main residential section is a school and two small stores (Fig. 14). Perhaps the location of most of the colonists on a dead-end road is a unifying factor, otherwise the nearest sociologically fusing center is northwestward at Pasmajärvi village.

The 1970 situation of the colony was a mixture of positive and negative elements. A few small areas of new clearing, two new farms, a new house (farm no. 28), well-kept appearances of some farmsteads, completion of the through road in the northern section of the major part, and milk platforms all the way to the south end of the road (Table 4) were encouraging. However, these were somewhat balanced by the absence of any electric power line, the vacancy of five houses in the eastern part of the northern section (Fig. 14 and Table 3), the main southern colony road being a dead-end type, only two stores and the school at the junction of the two colony roads, and a relatively small total area cleared and cropped. This may be generalized to a prognosis of an uncertain future.

Why has the evolution of Pasmajärven colony been slow? Probably for a number of reasons. Isolations, fragmentation of the colony, small farms, and lack of some facilities (e.g., social, religious, purchasing, and marketing) combine into a heavy load for any community. And the addition of the mixing of colonists and non-colonists at different times may have led to problems as a result of varying degrees of support by premiums or other compensation.

Financial costs may be part of the answer, also. By 1960 road construction costs in the colony had reached 38,600,000 FMK, a relatively high figure for the number of people there. Drainage costs by then were an additional 3,170,000 FMK, a relatively low figure (and probably related to the limited clearing in the colony). Even though a farmer generally paid only 5-10% of these charges they may

Table 3. Settling Characteristics of the Finnish MFZ Sample Colonies to Mid-Summer 1960*

Characteristic	Pasma-järven	Väli-joen	Kapusta-vuoman	Lisma-aavan	Urri-aavan
Location from Rovaniemi					
Direction	NW	S	WSW	NNE	E
Distance, Str. Line, Km.	83	32	65	90	152
Distance, Road, Km.	128	38	82	106	176
Date planned	1946	1951	1952	1953	1955
No. of farms	15	49	29	40	18
No. of persons/farm					
Mean	(5)	(7)	(4)	(7)+	6
Range	(2)	(8)	(0)	(13)	10
Farm size (hectares)					
Mean	105	218	275	213	221
Range	90	180	240	150	120
Arable land/farm (hectares)					
Mean	21	28	36	29	31
Range	24	30	32	18	28
Forest#/farm (hectares)					
Mean	66	144	173	162	145
Range	40	120	140	100	60
No. of months between contract signing and start of building construction					
Mean	45	28	6	10	7
Range	101	52	14	37	16
No. of months to build:					
Resid., Mean	32	12	10	10	11
Resid., Range	63	21	18	18	21
Sauna, Mean	23	10	6	3	12
Sauna, Range	49	37	27	8	36
Barn, Mean	32	14	22	5	9
Barn, Range	54	14	35	4	10
No. of parcels with:					
Resid., Sauna, & Barn	6	12	23	15	18
Resid. & Sauna	2	8	3	8	
Resid. only	2	4	2	8	
Resid. & Barn (& Outhse.)	2	9	1	5	
Sauna, or Barn, or Outhse.		3			
No Residence	4	25		4	

Table 3. (Continued)

Characteristic	Pasma-järven	Väli-joen	Kapusta-vuoman	Lisma-aavan	Urri-aavan
No. of farms bought	1	10	14	3	0
No. of farms w/cold farm## prem.	5	33	20	25	18
No. of farms w/clearing prem.				35	
No. of farms w/forest sales	9	37	26	36	17
No. of farms w/extended contract	6	33	4	14	17
No. of farms w/changed ownership	3	19		1	

* These data are from several sources but primarily from the Ministry of Colonization, Lapland Office, Rovaniemi. Grateful appreciation is extended to Fil. Lic. Lars Johnsson, formerly of the Stockholm School of Economics, for the collation and analyses of the data after the collection of them in the field.

+ Figures in parentheses are only suggested means because of the incompleteness of the data.

\# No allowances are made here for differences in quality of the various stands of forest in a farm. The parcels of forest in each farm are located, sized, and shaped on the basis of quality of the trees so as to distribute this resource evenly and in relation to the amount of arable land.

\## Cold farm refers to a new farm created entirely on land in its natural state.

have been too heavy a burden when added to the purchase price of a farm. Even though the settlers under Law 110 were not supposed to receive premiums for clearing land there apparently was at least some compensation for it (Table 4). But analysis of the premium and loans paid under the various acts used in Pasmajärven indicates that a major weakness there may have been too widely differing amounts of aid (and perhaps too little) to people in the same community.

Still, the settling began for general reasons other than economy. It all started in a time of national stress. But at Pasmajärven only a few of the northern Finns so sorely afflicted were included. And this may have been mostly a function of its great distance from the Soviet border where all the strain was focused. What is needed now is a careful sociological and psychological survey of the migrational attitudes of at least Pasmajärven's 11 original settlers still there to determine why the colony's development has been so slow.

Välijoen Colony

Valijoen Colony is situated in the central southern part of Lapland's Middle Fringe Zone. In addition to a lower regional isolation than Pasmajärven it is especially interesting because it is representative of how a larger-than-average colony was designed in the early 1950s to have many geographic and economic advantages. These the planners thought would lead quickly to viability but numerous early changes in ownership and recent signs of little farming have dampened their enthusiasm. The story of Välijoen is one of spotty growth in both time and internal geography.

This may hardly be blamed on lack of accessibility. The colony is just 38 km. (24 mi.) south of Rovaniemi by road, of which two-thirds is on Route 78; only 22 km. (14 mi.) westward on another two-lane, treated, graveled road is Route 926 following the east side of the Kemi River.[4] Thus, train and air service are available in one to two directions within 40 km. (25 mi.) and buses are run daily through and near the colony. Settlement patterns of long lines and groups of clusters of homes emphasize a low degree of local isolation. Further, its internal circulation pattern is one of almost completely through roads that are generally focused near the central point of the settled part of the colony (Fig. 15).

The physical base of the colony is one of the better in Lapland. In elevation the residential southern part is relatively low; its east-central section is a gently rolling morainic surface 120-130 meters (394-426 feet) above sea level while the remainder is drained swamp (Fig. 16) at 110-120 meters (361-394 feet)[5], both inside a westward

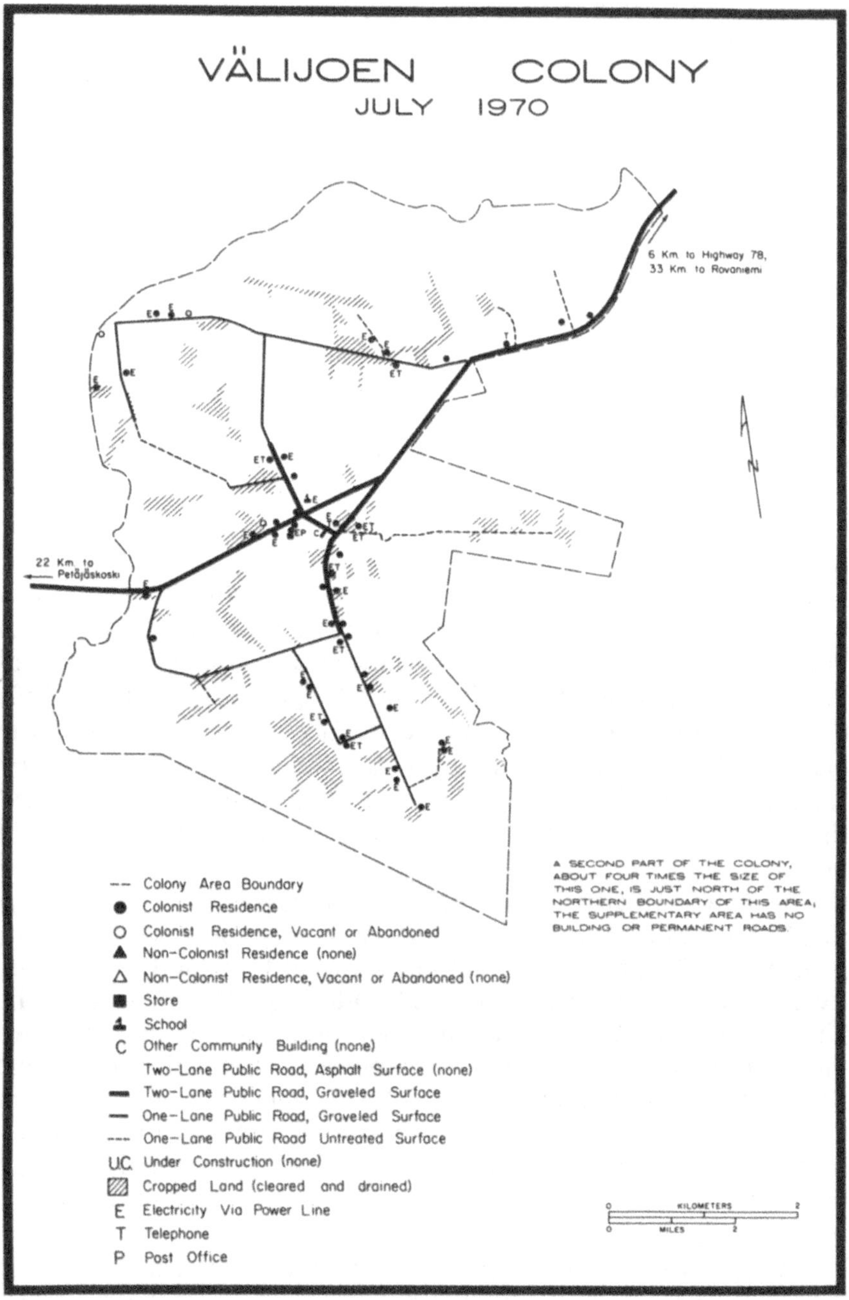
VÄLIJOEN COLONY
JULY 1970
6 Km to Highway 78,
33 Km to Rovaniemi
22 Km to
Petäjäskoski
A SECOND PART OF THE COLONY, ABOUT FOUR TIMES THE SIZE OF THIS ONE, IS JUST NORTH OF THE NORTHERN BOUNDARY OF THIS AREA; THE SUPPLEMENTARY AREA HAS NO BUILDING OR PERMANENT ROADS.
Colony Area Boundary
Colonist Residence
Colonist Residence, Vacant or Abandoned
Non-Colonist Residence (none)
Non-Colonist Residence, Vacant or Abandoned (none)
Store
School
C Other Community Building (none)
Two-Lane Public Road, Asphalt Surface (none)
Two-Lane Public Road, Graveled Surface
One-Lane Public Road, Graveled Surface
One-Lane Public Road Untreated Surface
U.C. Under Construction (none)
Cropped Land (cleared and drained)
E Electricity Via Power Line
T Telephone
P Post Office
0 KILOMETERS 2
0 MILES 2

Figure 15.

swing of the Vähäjoki River. But the uninhabited and larger northern part rises northwestward from the river to a bed-rock hill, Perunkavaara, that is 257 meters (843 feet) high and near the colony's NW corner; this part is entirely a birch-Scotch pine-spruce forest near a local drainage divide. Nearly all of the soils in the southern part were classed in 1951 as good in quality while those north of the river ranged from good to fair.[6]

Välijoen was started in June 1951. Though this was six years after the colonizing program began several of the original colonists are reported to have been DPs from the Petsamo district on the Arctic Ocean and some officials felt that persons who were mostly fishermen should not have been put into agricultural situations. Perhaps not. But development at Välijoen was delayed by poor timing of the construction of roads and ditches. The former were started in 1950 but were not completed until 1955; at that time ditches were started and were not finished until 1957. This could explain the 19 departures of colonists by 1960, highest for the sample colonies (Table 3), and two more in the next year. Certainly things moved slowly in the colony's first nine years; about 20% of its farms were bought but three-fourths of the contracts had to be extended (not an unusual action) while cold farm premium numbers were high and forest sales extensive (Table 3). Colonists were taking in money but there were not as many signs of permanence of settlement as some officials hoped for.

There were 49 farms and 12 homesites planned. Roads were laid out in a rough H shape with the homesites and school at the center; then the ends of the H were closed and two more small loops added (Fig. 15). Thus every home is on a through road, providing for relatively efficient use of milk trucks and school buses. Yet it is clear that a major N-S concentration of residences across the middle of the colony was planned for as well as a small central hamlet-type cluster. This left seven locally isolated farms in the NW (where three were vacant and one undeveloped in 1970), seven more rather widely spaced in the north (where three original settlers remain, two places appeared to have little farming in 1970, and one was above average in appearance then), and three in the west (where one remained undeveloped) (Fig. 15, Table 5).

Within the central cluster are some community services. There is a school, a small store, and, in the residence of farm no. 44 banking and postal facilities; nearby to the southeast is a small community building (Fig. 15). Interestingly there is no church, as is true at Päsmajarvi, but it appears that there might be enough people to support one in the Välijoen Colony and surrounding area. Apparently the planners' intentions were to have central services in 12 small plots along the NW/SE road at the colony center;[7] excepting the school such development has been at right angles southwestward to this and further growth appears likely in this same area.

Farm sizes were about average for Lapland colonies. The mean total in 1960, and there has been no change since because of restrictions against it, was 218 hectares (639 acres or 1 sq. mi.) of which 28 hectares (69 acres) were arable and 144 hectares (356 acres) were in forest (Table 3); ranges were modest and the remaining land was classed as useless (Table 5).

Figure 16. Välijoen Colony, fields. (See p. 94).

The principal crop land is in hay. It is scattered on the drained swamp in the western and northern sections of the colony's southern part (Fig. 15). Specialty crops, like vegetables for commercial markets (Fig. 16), are no longer grown in such quantities. In 1970 only 14 farms had milk pickup facilities and at just two places was new land being cleared. In fact, though most farms had power-line electricity (rather than the battery-power type common at Pasmajärven) and 10 had telephones, there were many where fields were uncropped and barns unused (Fig. 17).

On the other hand several places in the colony were quite viable in 1970. The presence of equipment, cars, power lines, telephones, carefully cropped fields, cleared ditches, and well-maintained buildings demonstrated the point. Their scattered locations showed these to be more reflections of individual traits than some overall physical or economic element of the landscape.

Figure 17. Välijoen Colony, farmstead. (See p. 94).

Several items may be related to this spotty development. The previously-noted poor timing of road and ditch construction was responsible for some delay. The large early turn-over of original settlers not only needs explanation but its effect on the colony's progress requires study. It is notable that several Petsamo DPs were said to be original settlers but most contemporary occupants settled under War Service provisions (Table 5). Official records also show that there were major differences in total subsidies allowed different settlers and certainly the use of cold farm premiums by 1960 shows wide differences that may demonstrate more than individual initiative and discipline. Further, it is possible that the location and accessibility of Välijoen Colony may have contributed to its uneven growth in time and area; being so close to Rovaniemi may have been more attractive recently for commuting to urban work rather than farming. This has been a trend throughout Finland's area with cities for at

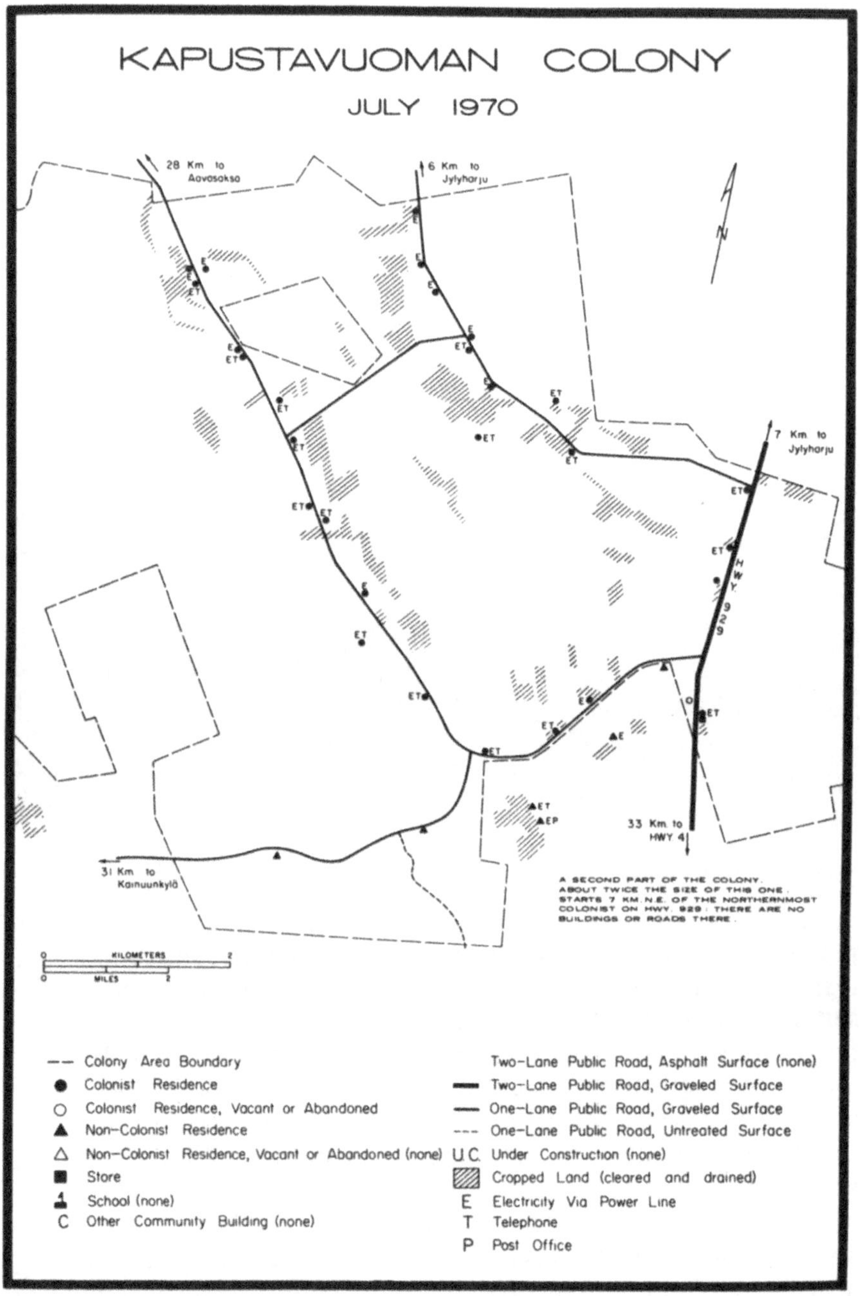
KAPUSTAVUOMAN COLONY
JULY 1970
28 Km to Aavasaksa
6 Km to Jylyharju
7 Km to Jylyharju
HWY. 929
33 Km to HWY 4
31 Km to Kainuunkylä
A SECOND PART OF THE COLONY, ABOUT TWICE THE SIZE OF THIS ONE, STARTS 7 KM. N.E. OF THE NORTHERNMOST COLONIST ON HWY. 929. THERE ARE NO BUILDINGS OR ROADS THERE.
KILOMETERS
MILES
Colony Area Boundary
Colonist Residence
Colonist Residence, Vacant or Abandoned
Non-Colonist Residence
Non-Colonist Residence, Vacant or Abandoned (none)
Store
School (none)
C Other Community Building (none)
Two-Lane Public Road, Asphalt Surface (none)
Two-Lane Public Road, Graveled Surface
One-Lane Public Road, Graveled Surface
One-Lane Public Road, Untreated Surface
U.C. Under Construction (none)
Cropped Land (cleared and drained)
E Electricity Via Power Line
T Telephone
P Post Office

Figure 18.

least two decades[8] and with the recent field reservation program, noted in Chapter 3, only the largest actively farmed units may be expected to remain in production in Välijoen. Here again an analysis in depth of the psychological and sociological make-up of the colony is most desirable, especially inasmuch as one might expect a proposal for establishment of some industry at such a location.

Kapustavuoman Colony

One of Lapland's more successful colonies is Kapustavuoman. Its status is the result of several favorable elements of colonizing, some of which may have been due to its start in the early 1950s or to its average size. In general, although its regional and local isolations are similar to those of Välijoen the overall development of Kapustavuoman Colony has been much steadier and more rapid and its original settlers have attained one of the higher degrees of permanence of rural settlement in the province.

In accessibility the colony is rather well off. Although it is 82 km. (51 mi.) from Rovaniemi by road the direction is west-southwest placing Kapustavuoman only 74 km. (46 mi.) north of the major city of Kemi (about 30,000 inhabitants). This may be reached by a direct road using Route 929 that runs along the eastern side of the colony or by an indirect one using Route 930, at the colony's northern end, which goes westward about 25 km. (15 mi.) to Aavasaksa on the Tornio River, the Swedish border. At the latter are bus and possible freight train services while at Kemi there are planes, trains, ships (in summer), and buses regularly and often. In this southwestern corner of Lapland rural settlement is densest, homes being in patterns of long lines, clusters, and even some small interrupted areas all making the local isolation low. In addition the internal circulation is one of alternative through single-lane gravel roads; the residential part is NW-SE about 10 km. (6 mi.) with two roads roughly parallel and 2 1/2 km. (1 1/2 mi.) apart that are connected in the middle and then at the ends by the aforementioned state routes (Fig. 18).

Kapustavuoman's physical features are quite favorable for colonizing. The residential and cropped part is mainly a flat grassy swamp between hills on the northern and southern sides; the latter rise to about 175 meters (574 feet) while the swamp elevations are 110-120 meters (361-394 feet).[9] Much of the northern road is in the characteristic location of the break between morainic soils with birch-Scotch-pine cover and the swamp (Fig. 19) while the southern road is partly this, in reverse orientation, and partly a route connecting low morainic knobs in the swamp (Fig. 20). Thus, each farmstead has the access by road, is where timber is immediately available, and is where vegetables and grains may be raised. In addition, as at Välijoen, there is a second part of the colony to the north for forestry; it is about 8 km. (5 mi.) away and has one parcel for each of the 29 farms. The significance of this part of Kapustavuoman and the early activity of its settlers were shown by all but three of the farms having significant timber sales by 1960 (Table 3).

Figure 19. Kapustavuoman Colony, farmstead. (See p. 94).

The colony's start in December 1952 also was advantageous. This was late enough for the planning to have profited from both previous mistakes and less hurried action. Probably the rapid early growth of the colony reflected several favorable elements of colonizing but it appears that the suitable physical features and access were taken advantage of by efficient planning and ambitious original settlers in combination with proper timing of general and specific actions, particularly construction of drainage ditches and roads and the provisions of settler financing. Also, some of this degree of success is attributable to the colony being average in number of farms in Lapland colonization and to the fact that the state owned much of the land in that location (Table 2).

Kapustavuoman's development was quick and steady. The construction time for saunas, homes, and barns was so much less than at Välijoen that the usual order of building (i.e., sauna the first year, etc.) was not followed and the time required for raising homes and saunas was 2-4 months shorter (Table 3). Swamp lands were broken and into production in relatively large amounts in the early years (Fig. 20) so cold farm premiums were largely used up by 1960 (Table 6). Only a few settlers requested extension of contracts (Table 3) and, in fact, all but farm no. 14 was purchased by 1964 (Table 6).

And this pattern of growth continued. By 1970 an even more permanent status appeared to have been reached. At that time 28 of

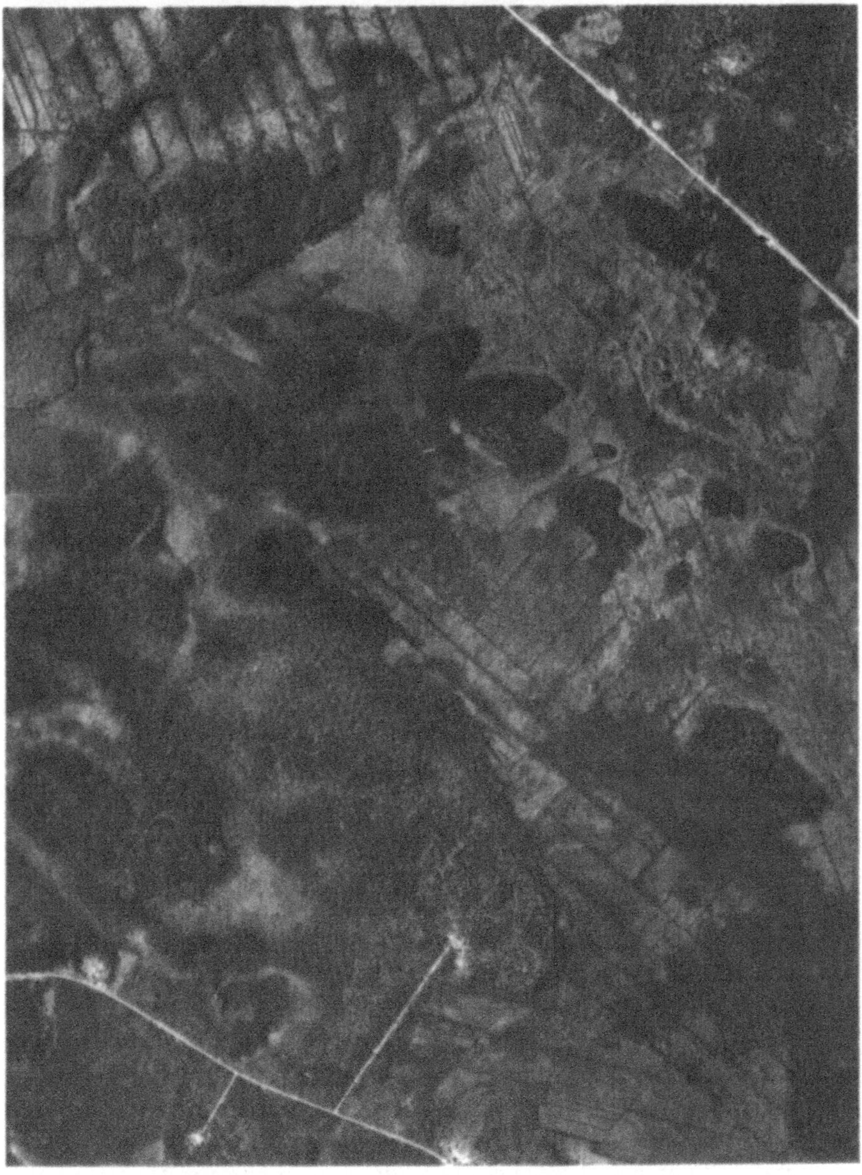

Figure 20. Kapustavuoman Colony, overview. (See p. 94).

the 29 farms were occupied by the original settlers; only farm no. 14 was not and it has, for some reason, been a problem since the colony's start. Nor had there been any changes in the original farm allotments.[10] Further, only two farms appeared not to be in full use at that time, 24 were sending out milk and/or cream, only two did not have electric power lines, and 17 had telephones (Fig. 18 and Table 6). Clearly the original settlers at Kapustavuoman were determined and the numerous buildings per farmstead and the nice appearance of many of them (Fig. 19) as well as of the fields are signals that intentions remain the same.

It is interesting that the colony has no centralized community services. Possibly the need has not developed because a minimum is present, mostly in the nearby small hamlet of Jylyharju (Fig. 18). At the road junction there a general store and bar are combined with a residence, nearby is a school and across from it a residence with postal facilities. Otherwise there are three farmsteads. Southward on Route 929 and almost out of the colony is another small grocery outlet in the residence of farm no. 13. But, like in the previous two colonies, there is no church or other organized forms of "sociological cement."

Perhaps there was a bit more arable land and a slightly higher value per farm at Kapustavuoman than at Välijoen. But the difference is not so great as the apparent greater degree of permanence of settlement at Kapustavuoman. Not only did original settlers do more, faster, and more permanently there but it was in spite of a location where the rural-urban migrational trend should have been about as great as possible in Lapland. Why? All signs clearly point first to some qualities of the settlers and, secondly, to planning and timing by administrators. This combination of the right people at the proper time in the correct place should be investigated thoroughly as soon as possible. In Kapustavuoman lie some possible major positive aids for future colonizing.

Lisma-aavan Colony

One of the more puzzling developments in Lapland is Lisma-aavan Colony. In 1970 it appeared to have weakening promise as an area of rural settlement but as one of the larger colonies begun in 1953 its future was auspicious. Though its regional isolation was high and its local isolation moderate to low the initial building and clearing was rapid, as at Kapustavuoman. Growth continued through the 1960s but by the end of the decade farming activity appeared greatly reduced and detracted from some signs of permanence of settlement.

Lisma-aavan has one of the higher degrees of isolation of a Lapland

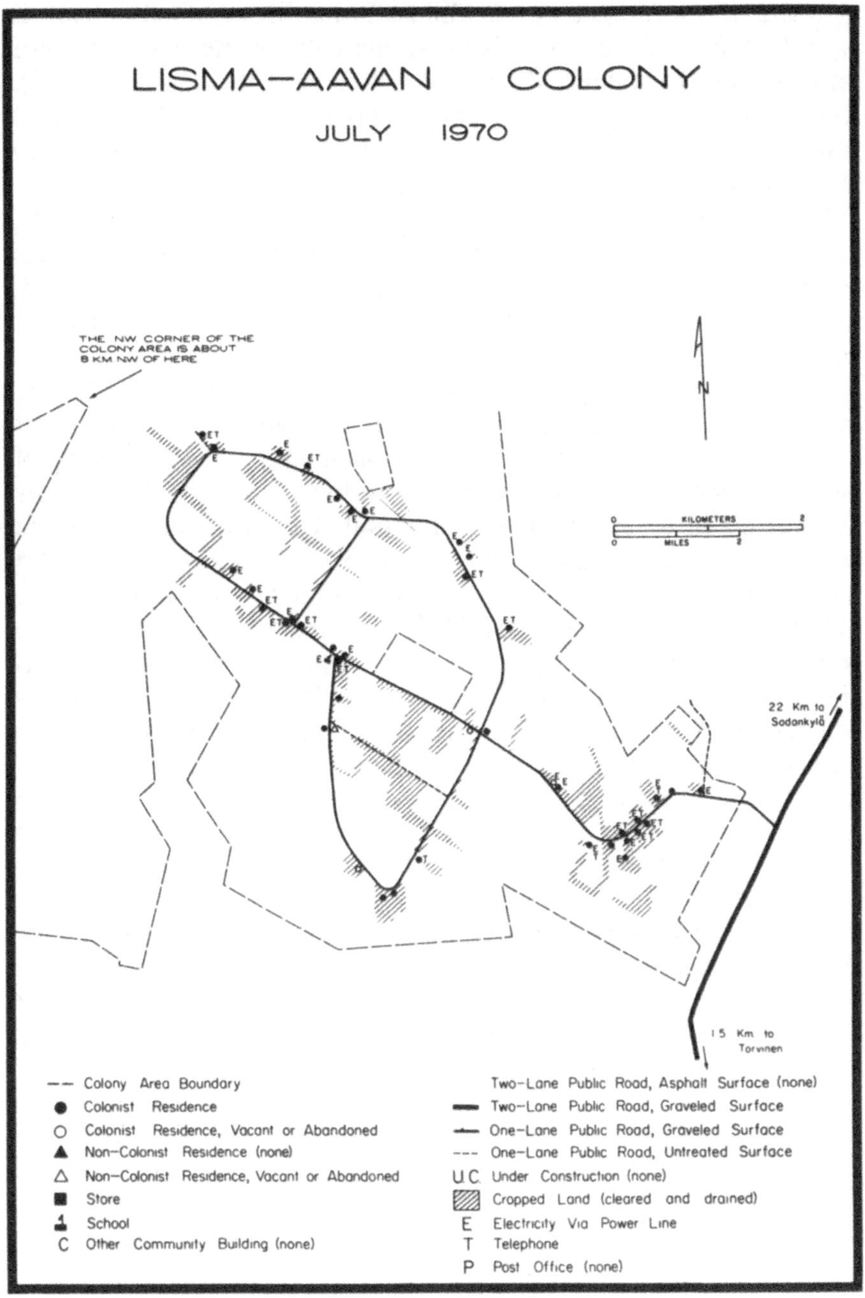
LISMA–AAVAN COLONY
JULY 1970
THE NW CORNER OF THE COLONY AREA IS ABOUT 8 KM NW OF HERE
N
KILOMETERS
MILES
22 Km to Sodankylä
15 Km to Torvinen
Colony Area Boundary
Colonist Residence
Colonist Residence, Vacant or Abandoned
Non-Colonist Residence (none)
Non-Colonist Residence, Vacant or Abandoned
Store
School
C Other Community Building (none)
Two-Lane Public Road, Asphalt Surface (none)
Two-Lane Public Road, Graveled Surface
One-Lane Public Road, Graveled Surface
One-Lane Public Road, Untreated Surface
U.C. Under Construction (none)
Cropped Land (cleared and drained)
E Electricity Via Power Line
T Telephone
P Post Office (none)

Figure 21.

colony. Being 106 km. (66 mi.) NNE of Rovaniemi its settlers are near the northern edge of the Middle Fringe Zone of settlement; it is, in fact, one of the larger-than-average colonies near the northern limit of the 61 established since World War II in Lapland (Fig. 2). Regionally the colony's entry and exit is at a point 22 km. (14 mi.) south of the village of Sodankylä on Route 4 and 1 km. (0.6 mi.) westward the district begins. From there on farther westward about 7 km. (4.3 mi.) the residential part extends with its single-lane, gravel roads in three loops (Fig. 21). Thus, there are alternative lines of movement within the colony but only one way in and out and, then, only two directions to go (north or south). In times of inclement weather or poor road conditions access is clearly limited.

Possibly the physical elements of the Lisma-aavan landscape are mixtures of favorable and not so good. Though the residential part of the colony, the southern half, was mapped in 1958 as capable of being cultivated,[11] the limits may be rather restrictive. The colony is, after all, at 67°15′ N. in a continental (versus marine) situation. Most of the cleared and cropped land is at elevations of 205-215 meters (672-705 feet) above sea level; immediately northward are hills with 320-350-meter (1050-1148-foot) crests while to the south is a swampland lining two rivers at the same 205 meters (672 feet) and some 4 km. (2 1/2 mi.) away are single hills of approximately 240 meters (787 feet).[12] There is, therefore, some question as to whether the southeastward air drainage is adequate in periods of hard frosts. Otherwise, the situation is the usual one in a north Finnish colony, that is, roads follow the breaks in slope between morainic soils and swamps, as in northern Lisma-aavan, or they run from one morainic knob to another, as in the rest of the colony. As in most of Lapland the better drained ridges support Scotch pine stands, the rest of the ridges spruce and birch (as in much of Lisma-aavan), and the swamps one to three types of vegetation. The latter in the Lisma-aavan lower areas is predominantly a higher-quality grassland which is easily cleared and makes good land for hay.

Starting the colony in May 1953 provided similar advantages to those at Kapustavuoman. Planners had had the experience in selecting land, people, financial programs, road and drainage systems, and farm layouts. At Lisma-aavan the initial designs appeared suitable; most farms were in two or three parcels within a single colonization district[13] (unlike Päsmajarven and Kapustavuoman), roads were looped, farmsteads were beside a road and on morainic soils, and mean farm sizes and subdivisions into arable and forest land were similar to Välijoen (Table 3). Special steps in settler selection are reported.[14]

But there were variations in the internal details of some of these. The farmsteads were really in four groups with that to the south having a higher degree of local isolation than the rest (Fig. 21). The farms were a little smaller than at Välijoen and Kapustavuoman but, more important, had wide local differences; there was no standard size of unit. Arable areas, for example, ranged from 22 to 36 1/2 hectares (54-90 acres), wooded ones from 108 to 195 hectares (267-482 acres), and, worst of all, useless areas from 0.5 to 121 hectares (1.2-300 acres) (Table 7). How these may have affected the present-day situation is yet to be learned.

Certainly the colonists got off to a fast start. Most building was begun in less than a year from the time of signing of contracts, much less than at Välijoen but not so at two other colonies (Table 3). Further, construction time for homes was as short as at Kapustavuoman but for saunas and barns the lowest of the five sample colonies.

By mid-1960 the colony generally was growing fast. Some 36 homes were constructed and several were painted, the school was in operation, ditches were in, stump rows were burning at the edges of newly cleared morainic fields, wood was being cut and sold at nearly every farm, and clearing and cold farm subsidies were being paid out rapidly (Fig. 22). On the other hand, though, by that time only 3

Figure 22. Lisma-aavan Colony, farmstead. *(See p. 94).*

farms had been bought, 14 had had contract extensions, 1 had changed ownership and two more were about to change. Moreover, several of the homes were sited quite differently from the planners' locations.[15] Another sign of variations was in the cold farm premium used at each farm by 1960; this ranged from 32% of a small allowance to 95% of large ones (Table 7). In addition, 35 farms had special premiums for clearing (Table 3) and within Lisma-aavan special loans were being made for electricity (usually 80,000-100,000 FMK). The government was clearly pushing for development and under such conditions variations in individual management often become apparent. Differences within the colony were developing.

By the summers of 1963 and 1964 wide ranges in effort were obvious. Some farmsteads had been pushed to completion, painted, and landscaped (Fig. 23) while others were of plain weathered boards in the midst of farmyard rubble. Some 14 places had electric power lines and 2 had telephones. At a few fields smoldering fires marked continued efforts to clear land but in others hay cocks and racks were idle and fields and drains unkempt. The general effect was of continued progress (Fig. 24) but specific ones varied.

Figure 23. Lisma-aavan Colony, farmstead. *(See p. 94).*

By the summer of 1970 the aspect of Lisma-aavan Colony had changed. It appeared rather lifeless in several spots and ways. Two farms were still undeveloped (nos. 1 and 41), 4 farmsteads were vacant (Fig. 25), there was little or no farming or only recreational use at 15 farms, and only 6 milk or cream pick-up stands (Table 7). Still original settlers owned or were present at 32 of the units, electric power lines went to 30 farmsteads, telephones were at 14, and additions of buildings or cleared land were under way at 4. Though there were large areas of cleared land throughout the colony (Fig. 21) much was unused, particularly inside the southern road loop (where, also, the transverse road was no longer passable all the way). Nor were there many signs of woods work other than between farmsteads 15 and 24 (the eastern part of the northern road).

Figure 24. Lisma-aavan Colony, overview. (See p. 94).

In a colony so large and with higher degrees of isolation Lisma-aavan might have been expected to have some kind of community center. Particularly with its road pattern. But such was and is not the case. Two small "cooperative areas" and three special homesites were designated on the original plans.[16] However, these were scattered all over and only the combination store and residence was established at the central road junction (as unit no. 43). By 1970 nothing else was at this point but a vacant two-building farmstead and at that time much of the colony was served by a traveling store from Sodankylä. The school, at the next road junction westward, was the only other community facility present. Why no center was planned for a district of 41 farms is unknown.[17]

Lisma-aavan Colony's future is not clear. If the reduction in farming during the late 1960s was primarily a result of the field reservation program then concern for the colony's coming years should be great. The people and farms are where they are because of the suitability of the grassland for agriculture. The colony has high degrees of isolation and no alternative occupations but lumbering. There appears little to hold the colonists together as a unit even if there are enough younger ones desirous of doing it. An observer senses in Lisma-aavan that more than usual its outlook depends on the attitudes of its people. A study of them may disclose alternatives for the future that are not yet recognized.[18]

Figure 25. Lisma-aavan Colony, farmstead. *(See p. 94).*

Urriaavan Colony

Like Kapustavuoman, Urriaavan Colony is one of Lapland's more successful. Though it has high degrees of isolation, is smaller than average, and was one of the last colonies established, it developed at average speeds in some respects; in others growth was fast. But in permanence of settlement it is the most accomplished of the five sample colonies and is an excellent example of determination of colonists.

Urriaavan is highly isolated. Regionally it is in the extreme southeastern corner of Lapland 176 km. (109 mi.) by road east of Rovaniemi, just 23 km. (14 mi.) from the Soviet border, 56 km. (36 mi.)

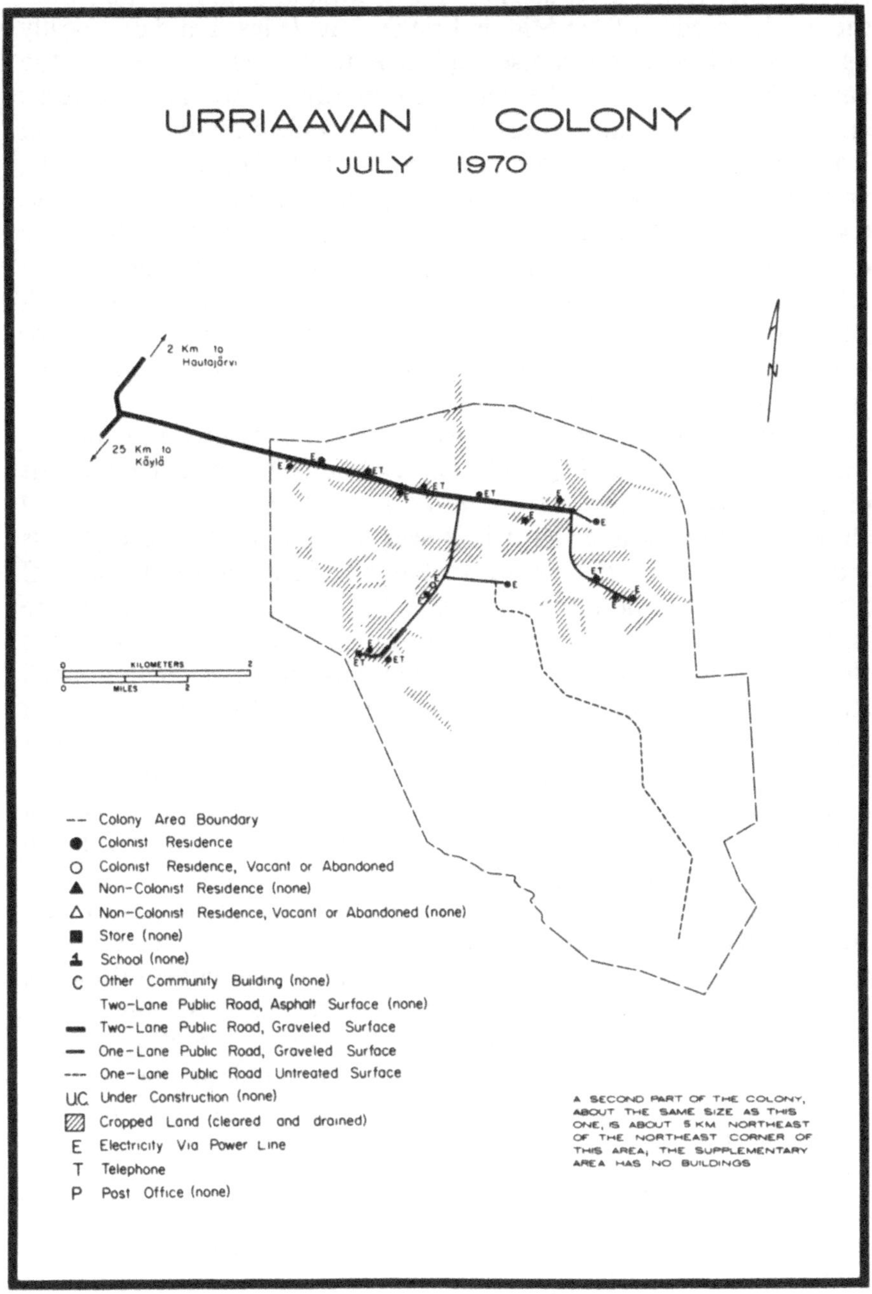
URRIAAVAN COLONY
JULY 1970
2 Km to Hautajärvi
25 Km to Käylä
KILOMETERS
MILES
-- Colony Area Boundary
● Colonist Residence
○ Colonist Residence, Vacant or Abandoned
▲ Non-Colonist Residence (none)
△ Non-Colonist Residence, Vacant or Abandoned (none)
■ Store (none)
School (none)
C Other Community Building (none)
Two-Lane Public Road, Asphalt Surface (none)
Two-Lane Public Road, Graveled Surface
One-Lane Public Road, Graveled Surface
One-Lane Public Road Untreated Surface
UC Under Construction (none)
Cropped Land (cleared and drained)
E Electricity Via Power Line
T Telephone
P Post Office (none)
A SECOND PART OF THE COLONY, ABOUT THE SAME SIZE AS THIS ONE, IS ABOUT 5 KM NORTHEAST OF THE NORTHEAST CORNER OF THIS AREA; THE SUPPLEMENTARY AREA HAS NO BUILDINGS

Figure 26.

north of the town of Kuusamo, and less than 50 km. (31 mi.) from the northern edge of the Middle Fringe Zone (Figs. 1 and 6). Locally its degree of isolation is also high making the area more like the Outer Fringe Zone of settlement than the MFZ. Settlement patterns are spots and short lines (Fig. 7). One can move only north-south on Route 950, a two-lane gravel road connecting Kuusamo and Salla, or westward on Route 948 from Hautajärvi, a small village about 6 km. (4 mi.) north of Urriaavan's center. Entry to and exit from the colony is by just one E-W road, two lanes wide but used only in the middle, which narrows internally to two southward, one-lane, dead-end routes (Fig. 26). Thus, settlers have no alternative ways for circulation and nearly the bare minimum in number of neighbors and connections with them.

In physical elements of the landscape the colony is generally suitable for a hay-based agriculture. Elevations in the residential part of the colony are a few meters above or below 240 meters (787 feet) above sea level; where lower it is swamp land and where higher is ground moraine and the highest spot in the area is a hill at the turn-off from Route 950 where the summit is 299 meters (980 feet).[19] There is, therefore, less relief here than in much of Lapland. Drainage is slowly southeastward via ditches emptying into two nearby small streams. The swampy areas are the grassy type, rated as good for cultivation,[20] while the slightly higher and drier spots have a cover of birch and Scotch pine. The main colony road follows a poorly defined higher area and the two southern tributaries reach to higher and drier parts so that farmsteads may be in the usual north Finnish position of change in slope and soil.

When the colony was started in February 1955 some 18 farms were laid out. These averaged 221 hectares (546 acres) but were valued somewhat less than farms in the other sample colonies (Table 8). Nearly every farm was composed of three parcels; one was for the farmstead and hay fields near the colony roads, a second was immediately to the south in morainic land penetrated by a lumbering track, and a third in the separate and lumbering-only section of the colony to the northeast.[21] Nearly all farms were entered at the same time and most of the colonists were former servicemen.

Urriaavan got off to a fast start. At most farms the sauna was started first but the residence commonly was begun at nearly the same time; most barns were started in 1958 (Table 8). Each type of building was completed in less than a year (long for the sauna and average for the residence but short for the barn; Table 3) so it is clear that colonists moved to farming quickly. Within 5 years most colonists had used upwards of two-thirds or more of their premiums for

Figure 27. Urriaavan Colony, fields. (See p. 94).

clearing and all but one family was busy at timber cutting for income. Thus, by mid-1960 every home was up and many were painted, clearing was in progress at at least 7 farms, and much ditching was done. It is true on the other hand, that there were no milk stands, no electric power lines, no telephones, and roads were of loose sand and gravel.

In addition, there was no community center and no community services were available internally. The nearest were in the village of Hautajärvi where there was a school, 3 stores, 2 churches, and a post office. Perhaps this suffices for a colony of Urriaavan's size and with its location for by 1970 the provision of community services was still the same.

By 1960, though, the colonists had developed a momentum that was not to be lost (Fig. 27). It was too soon to expect completion of farm purchase by then; still by 1963 most farms were bought or nearly so and the average buying time was a short one of 8-9 years (Table 8). In the same year vertical air photos disclosed new land being cleared in both swamps and higher land and recent cutting in the timbered parcels.[22] It was obvious on every hand that, as one local Finnish official said, "They are all hard workers, those people!".

The 1970 aspect of Urriaavan also supported that compliment. By then cleared land was all over the colony in large blocks (Fig. 26). Fences were up and farmsteads generally well kept (Fig. 28). Several families had a car. Every farm had an electric power line and 6 had telephones (Table 8). At least 9 farms sent out milk or cream and others had herds for family needs. At only 2 farms was the use of fields incomplete and the one vacant farmstead (no. 14) was clearly just temporarily not in use.

Figure 28. Urriaavan Colony, farmstead. (See p. 94).

As at Lisma-aavan, Urriaavan Colony's future appears to depend primarily upon the settlers' initiative and effort. Excepting that at Urriaavan the future appears bright and promising. This in spite of high degrees of isolation and without the community services that some planners consider essential. Why? As usual, colonizing is by and for the settlers – if they believe they can settle in an area and wish to they are likely to succeed in spite of elements that are disadvantageous. It is this spirit that must be both sought and measured for without it the best laid plans may not survive.

General Retrospection

Lapland's settlement has been quite dynamic since 1940. Nor has it stopped. During the war-time period two types of destruction occurred, 1) that associated directly with military action and 2) the spiteful retreat of the Nazi forces that were there. Then came the reverse. On top of the repair of war damage came the establishment of 61 agricultural-forestry colonies as well as many farmer-foresters settling singly; northern Finland became one of the world's few areas of rural settlement advancing on a regional scale into unsettled areas. By this growth in the 1950s and 1960s Lapland provided an interesting contrast with adjoining areas where local advancing took place in Norway[23] and regional-scale retreating occurred in inner northern Sweden.[24]

In general northern Finland's appearance is still one of growth. Cities and towns, especially Rovaniemi and Kemi, are expanding in several ways. And the rural aspect parallels this. More recently founded colonies still have parts in the earliest stages of "pioneering". For example, at Kaalamanniemen Colony (67°30′ N., just south of Muonio on Fig. 2) farmsteads were still being built in 1970, original clearing was being undertaken, the smaller drains were being established, and 14 of the proposed 25 farms were starting up; also in 1970 at the most recently founded colony (1967) of Haukijärvi-Taipole, just west of Välijoen, new roads were under construction and a few farms were being established. Signs of activity and expansion usually are more easily observed than the opposite but even cautious examination all over southern Lapland disclosed no more than the normal number of vacancies (not abandonment) on a rural landscape.

However, at the local scale some colonies had signs of developing problems. The slow growth and lack of common facilities at Pasmajärvi was one. At Välijoen the early departures of settlers and the contemporary spottiness of growth is another. And the outstanding third one is Lisma-aavan Colony where the recent sudden decline in farming and the abandonment of farms foreshadows a loss of viability.

Meanwhile two of the sample colonies offer considerable encouragement to planning for new rural settling. At Kapustavuoman most signs are of favorable combinations of the elements of colonizing and 18 years after founding the colony was steadily progressing. Similarly Urriaavan seemed to have one of the more secure futures when it was only 15 years old.

Why these differences? There are many reasons, of course. Variation of results is expectable when one adds different kinds of people to different kinds of landscapes at different times with different plans and different preparations. It has been stated so well in "The success of the process of development depends on the simultaneous operation of all the working parts of which it is composed."[25] But rural settling is hardly a series of actions that can be made into a regression analysis for computer processing to automatic success. To be sure, agriculture in Lapland requires "... careful management of a complex system ... precisely located ..."[26] yet varying degrees of permanence of settlement within a colony such as Välijoen and over time in one like Lisma-aavan is frustrating to planners. The lack of a community center might be used to explain some of the situation at Pasmajärven and Lisma-aavan, still there is none at the two more successful of the sample colonies, Kapustavuoman and Urriaavan. A geographer might add that locational advantages explain much of Kapustavuoman's status, to be challenged by a planner's claims about good timing and design, but how does each then explain Urriaavan's situation? The only generalization not yet disproved pertains to size: higher degrees of success are associated with colonies of 15-30 farms. Surely other elements must be added in correct proportions and at the proper times.

Meanwhile the need for more extended and sophisticated studies of the settlers is clearer than ever. Some authors have spoken to this recently by emphasizing that the "human engineering" lags behind the agricultural and civil engineering in analytical and predictive values for new settling.[27] Examination of the five sample Lapland colonies in some detail during a period of 15 years has led time and again to the conclusion that psychological and sociological studies of the settlers before, during, and after settling will provide the most useful results in the next stage of research on rural settling processes and rural settlement morphology. The challenge is truly multi-disciplinary.

NOTES TO CHAPTER 4

1. Maanmittaushallitus Lantmäteristyrelsen, *Suomen Tiekartta,* No. 12, Helsinki, Feb. 1970, scale 1/400,000.

2. Maanmittaushallituksen Kivipaino, *Pasmajärvi* (Map), No. 2642, 1961, scale 1/100,000.

3. ----, (Pasmajärven asutusaluetta), *Toimitus No. 4147,* 1946, scale 1/16,000; originals available at the national mapping agency archives in Rovaniemi.

4. Maanmittaushallitus ...., *op. cit.*

5. Maanmittaushallituksen Kivipaino, *Ahmarakka* and *Kakarijärvi* and *Kuusikkolamuri* (Maps), Nos. 3611 07, - 08, - 11, 1967, scale 1/20,000.

6. Rovaniemen valtionmaat., *Viljelykelpoisuuskartta,* Nos. 3611 07, - 08, - 09, 1951, scale 1/20,000.

7. Maanmittaushallituksen Kivipaino, (Välijoen asutusaluetta), *Toimitus No. 4390,* 1949-1951, scales 1/8000 and 1/16,000; originals available at the national mapping agency archives in Rovaniemi.

8. G. Beyer, *Rural Migrants in Urban Setting,* The Hague, 1963, pp. 141-152.

9. Maanmittaushallituksen Kivipaino, *Kapustavuoma* and *Mellakoski* and *Varejärvi* (Maps), Nos. 2631 05, -06, -08, -09, 1965, scale 1/20,000.

10. ----, Kartta Kapustavuoman asutusalueesta, *Toimitus No. 5524,* 1951, scale 1/16,000; originals available at the national mapping agency archives in Rovaniemi.

11. Tehty Maatalousministeriön, *Viljelyskelpoisuustutkimukset, Sodankylän kunnassa,* 1958, scale 1/400,000, Sodankylä (?).

12. Maanmittaushallituksen Kivipaino, *Aska* and *Juppurat* and *Torvinen* (Maps), Nos. 3713 07, -04, 3624 09, 1962, 1969, 1970 (resp.), scale 1/20,000.

13. ----, *Sodankylä kl. 4, Lisma-aapa,* 1952, scale 1/50,000.

14. G. H. Michie, Välijoki and Lisma: New Planned Settlements in Finnish Lapland, *Canadian Geographer,* v. V, 1961, pp. 24-36, ref. on p. 28.

15. Maanmittaushallituksen Kivipaino, (Lisma-aavan asutusalueesta), *Toimitus No. 4954,* 1952-1953, scale 1/8000; originals available at the national mapping agency archives in Rovaniemi.

16. *Ibid.,* sheet III.

17. The literature on the planning of centers is relatively large but a recent single publication covering many items referred to here is D. B. W. M. Van Dusseldorf, *Planning of Service Centres in Rural Areas of Developing Countries,* Publ. 15, Intern. Inst. Land Reclam. and Imprvmt., Wageningen, Netherlands, 1971.

18. A sociological study of the Lisma-aavan colonists was begun in 1970 by Mrs. Leena Alanen through the Department of Sociology at the University of Helsinki.

19. Maanmittaushallituksen Kivipaino, *Oulanka* and *Savinajoki* (Maps), Nos. 4612 10 and 4614 01, 1963, scale 1/20,000.

20. Tehty Maatalousministeriön, *Viljelyskelpoisuuskartta, Salla,* 1958 (?), scale 1/8000.

21. Maanmittaushallituksen Kivipaino, (Urriaavan asutusalueesta), *Toimitus No. 8333,* 1953-54, scale 1/8000; originals available at the national mapping agency archives in Rovaniemi.

22. Sortie 6330, pictures 65-69, taken August 1963, scale 1/60,000 and kindly made available for purchase through the Topographic Service of the Finnish Defense Force.

23. K. H. Stone, *Norway's Internal Migration to New Farms since 1920,* Euro. Demogr. Monogr., M. Nijhoff, The Hague, 1971.

24. K. H. Stone, Regional Abandoning of Rural Settlement in Northern Sweden, *Erdkunde,* v. XXV, 1971, pp. 36-51.

25. R. Weitz, *Rural Development in A Changing World,* Cambridge, Mass., 1971, p. 15.

26. C. J. W. Edward, Methods of Maintaining Settled Agriculture in Finnish Lapland, *Arctic,* v. 25, 1972, pp. 8-20.

27. K. H. Stone, Geographic Aspects of Planning for New Rural Settling in the Free World's Northern Lands in S. B. Cohen (ed.), *Problems and Trends in American Geography,* New York, 1967, pp. 221-238, ref. on p. 233; Z. Pioro, An Ecological Interpretation of Settlement Systems, *Intern. Soc. Sci. Jnl.,* v. XVIII, 1966, pp. 527-537; E. Glässer, Die ländlichen Siedlungen, *Geogr. Rundschau,* v. 21, 1969, pp. 161-180; W. Tietze, Current Tasks of Settlement Geography in View of Total Urbanisation, *Geoforum,* No. 3, 1970, pp. 39-46; M. Born, Zur Erforchung der ländlichen Siedlungen, *Geogr. Rundschau,* v. 22, 1970, pp. 369-374.

Chapter 5

NATIONAL AND NORTHERN FINNISH POPULATION CHANGES AND MIGRATIONS, 1969-1972

Now still another change is occurring in Lapland's demography. This is the contemporary loss of people. But it is a population trend that is somewhat different from that of the rest of the country. In the north total numbers reached a maximum in 1966 and have declined since whereas national totals peaked in 1970, declined, and then began a slight increase in 1972. A large part of these losses was directly related to emigration, primarily to Sweden; in the nation it took place mostly in 1970 but in Lapland it extended to weak showings in early 1972. Meanwhile the internal rural-urban shifting from earlier decades continued all over Finland. From these population trends and the detailed studies of the sample colonies it appears that the dynamics of the 1972 distribution of permanent residences are in delicate balance, making forecasts for long periods quite disputable. In fact, the future appears to be a time of declining total and rural populations and increasing numbers in the larger urban places.

National Population Trends

Finland's total population has had a worrisome course since the end of 1969.[1] In January 1970 a peak figure of 4,707,100 was reached. Then began the country's first peace-time population decline since the 19th-century famine. Slowly the numbers dropped to a first low of 4,677,000 in early 1971 (Fig. 29). Through the remainder of 1971 it was barely increasing to a November figure some 9000 higher. Then came further cause for concern. By December 1971 the contemporary low of 4,632,000 was recorded. From that time through the first six months of 1972 the new increase was a slow one of just 13,000 persons.

By July 1972 Finnish numbers were 4,647,000. This was still below the January 1970 high and well under what earlier forecasts had expected. But in 1971 and 1972 only slow growth could have been expected at best. The birth rate was then down to 13.7 per 1000

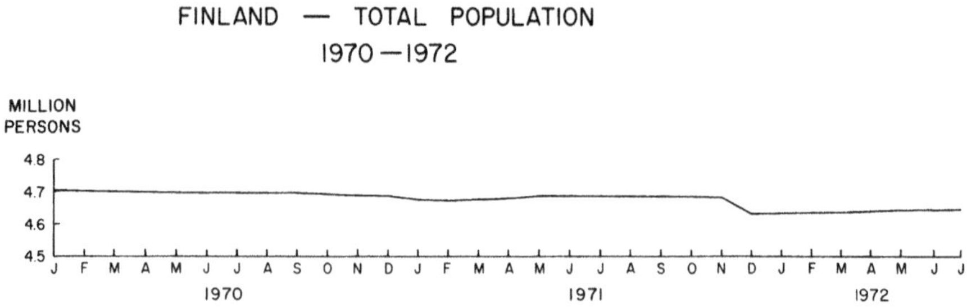

Figure 29.

and the death rate was 9.5 per 1000. Both were somewhat lower than the averages of births (16 and 15 per 1000) and deaths (11 per 1000) in northern and western Europe.[2] However, the Finnish growth rate of 0.4 per cent per year was the lowest, with Sweden, in northern Europe. This, of course, reflected emigrational strains as well as other elements of slow growth.

Such major changes in Finland's total population is a matter of concern to many people. For the Finns, a rightfully proud people, the drop in numbers of an already-small population is a threat to continued existence. But to the free world a challenge of Finland's survival is an item of major significance. The country is, after all, a truly democratic one adjoining the Soviet Union for nearly 1270 km. (788 mi.) and it is a nation which has demonstrated a continuing ability to live at peace, while maintaining trading relations, with both the Soviet and Western Worlds.[3] What other nation is in such a position of current and potential leadership? And if there is any, has it been strained so by recent emigration?

National Migrations

All Finland has been affected by an emigrational trend for several decades. Sweden has been the dominant attraction taking nearly half the émigrés in the 1950s and three-quarters of them between 1961 and 1965.[4] Just when an excess of out-migration started is unclear because the estimated losses in the first part of the 20th century were small. Between 1900 and 1945, for instance, the Finns residing in Sweden totalled only 3500-5500 in any year.[5] Further, between 1946 and 1954 the net migration usually was 3000-5000 a year; however, twice it exceeded 10,000 annually.

In 1954 all specific measures were stopped. The Nordic Council was formed then and a major purpose was to encourage the exchange of laborers between countries so citizens of Norden no longer needed passports and could not be counted. However, Majava's computations from Swedish population statistics showed that net Finnish emigration to Sweden from 1954 through 1963 averaged roughly 6500 a year but was more than 9000 in both 1960 and 1961.[6] Big losses were starting. They continued at more than 15,000 in 1964, 17,000 in 1965, 10,000 in 1966, and 11,000 in 1968.[7] In 1969, the beginning of the contemporary period, net emigration to Sweden exceeded 32,000 persons. Although that year was when Finland's total population peaked the drains of emigration were clear. Worries were legion. So special Finnish counting was begun in January 1970.

It was just in time. In 1970 some 45,565 Finns emigrated, the highest number ever (Fig. 30). By the year's end the total population was down to 4,683,000 and declining (Fig. 29). This continued through February and March 1971 as noted above. During these 15 months the maxima of emigration were nearly 5800 in September 1970 and about 4000 in the previous March (Fig. 30). In all the losses were more than 1500 per month until December 1970. In April 1971 Finland's out- and in-migration balanced. Incoming persons then outnumbered the outgoing through the summer but in the fall months of 1971 emigration was dominant again, though in small numbers. Since then, from October 1971 through June 1972 in-migration dominated and in those last three months was increasing (Fig. 30). Thus, in small-scale geographical considerations Finland's international emigrational current has reached its lowest strength in this century. The worry of declining numbers in this strategically-located part of the free world is, therefore, at least partially lightened.

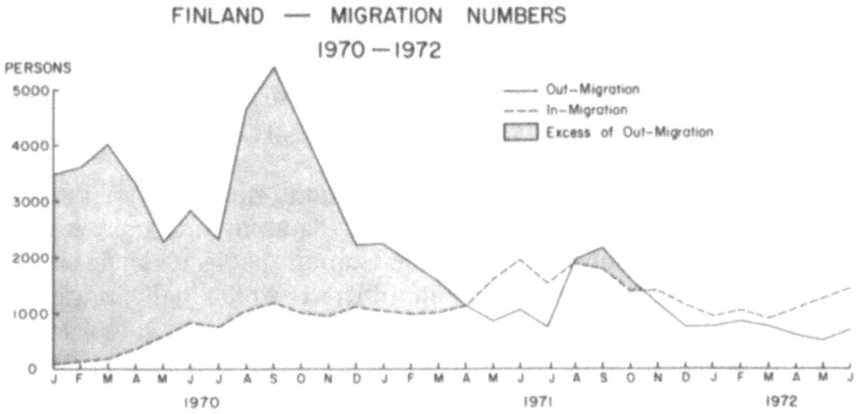

Figure 30.

Why did these movements take place? For a number of reasons. Sweden was the nearest well developed, neutral and free nation. In gross national product it was Europe's leader (and second only to the U.S.A.) in 1969 with a value of $2920 U.S.A. per capita, growing at 3.4 per cent per year, compared to Finland's $1980 U.S.A. and growing at 3.9 per cent per annum.[8] It was recently concluded that there are direct relationships, with a six-month lag, between the number of vacant jobs in Sweden and the number of Finnish emigrants.[9] Furthermore, Sweden is well known for having been neutral since 1809 (so many Finnish children were sent there for protection during World War II). Traditionally there are ties between the two nations because of an historic period of Swedish rule for six centuries and because Sweden is a democratic monarchy. Of course, there were additional internal forces of "push" behind emigration, such as, the field reservation program to discourage certain forms of agriculture. Under these circumstances one might expect, then, that the Finnish emigrants to Sweden since 1946 have been predominantly single adult males, single adult females, and children less than 15 years of age, usually in that order.[10] Also, rural persons led in emigration and immigration in 1970 and 1971 but in early 1972 there were more urbanites emigrating from Finland than ruralites and in in-migration persons of rural origins outnumbered those with urban residences.

National migrations also include another geographical current, namely, Finland's internal rural-urban migration. This has been a long-time movement but one that has accelerated since World War II. For example, at the beginning of the 20th century the country was predominantly rural and by 1959 only about 62 per cent of the population still was; but at the end of 1970 the urban numbers exceeded the rural 2,393,000 to 2,287,000.[11] This movement has been well documented and over and over one finds the biggest places, like Helsinki for the country and Rovaniemi for Lapland, getting bigger while the smallest places are either growing very slowly or declining.[12]

In fact, in 1963 official resistance to some directions of internal migration was generated. The National Planning Committee then reported "In its population study the Committee discovered that the direction of internal migration in Finland, which had during the centuries long period of settlement been from the south and south-west to the north, had gradually been reversed; the population had begun to migrate back to the areas populated first, or from the north and north-east to the south and south-west."[13] It went on with "The Committee felt that a migratory movement of such an order of magnitude from areas already sparsely populated, but capable of development, to the largest population centres was unwholesome from the point of view of the nation as a whole. Above all, it regarded this phenomenon as an indication that economic life had failed to develop sufficiently rapidly in some parts of the country and that the social conditions under which the population of the remote districts had to live were still marred by serious defects."[14] Several lines of remedial action were proposed and have been taken.

Economic developments, sponsored and otherwise, have encouraged rural-urban migration. Industrialization was accelerated after World War II to make treaty payments to the Soviet Union and, once this was done, was continued with emphasis on forest products industries. But in October 1965 a new national policy shifted the emphasis to machinery and design goods, especially for foreign trade.[15] This increased sophistication economically was demonstrated geographically by commune changes as follows: in 1950-1955 there were scattered population decreases in the southern half of Finland mixed with areas of population increase but migration loss, in 1956-1960 in most of southern Finland the communes lost population but a few had population increase in spite of migration loss, and in 1961-1965 nearly all of southern Finland's communes experienced population decrease – meanwhile the bigger cities grew all the time.[16] At the same time governmental actions to reduce the national problems of agricultural overproduction and uneconomic sizes of farms by such as the field reservation program[17] and high unemployment figures, especially in the north[18], have added impetus to internal movements of the Finns.

Northern Finland, Numbers

The National Planning Committee's distress in 1963 over southward migration from northern Finland was expressed even before the major recent losses of population. Finland's total numbers did not reach a peak until six years later and it was then that the country and the northern provinces of Oulu and Lapland were suffering the most.

During the 1970-1971 period the greatest international emigration by province was centered in the north. Oulu Province, which also had many post-war agricultural-forestry colonies, was the country's leader for seven months in 1970. In total and rural populations Oulu's provincial trends were somewhat similar to the country's; that is, maximum numbers were reached by 1966,[19] a few years before the national's, and its rural population has been decreasing since 1960 (Table 9).

Oulu's international migrational pattern also paralleled the country's. Big losses characterized 1970 with maxima of 1100-1150 a month in August and September; these were followed by small losses in just the fall of 1971 (Fig. 31). This trend was interesting geographically because the province is between Lapland, which adjoins Sweden, and Vaasa which includes a major emigrational port with respect to Sweden. However, in the first half of 1972 the international losses were being made up (Fig. 31). Still the signs of continued southward internal migration remained with declining total and rural populations (Table 9).

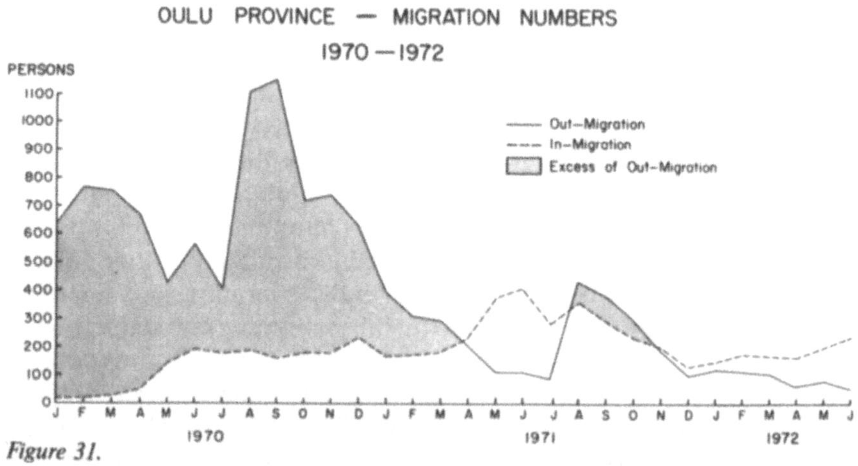

Figure 31.

Lapland's emigrational trends, however, have been mostly different from those in Oulu Province. The one similarity was a peak of total numbers in 1966, anticipated as 221,162.[20] But levels were maintained through 1968 when the drop was only 407 people and a major difference was an increase in the rural population (Table 9). Colonizing was still having its effect in Lapland. At that time the geographical counter-currents of incoming colonists versus outgoing Laplanders were in greatest contrast. But the latter were dominant for both total and rural populations declined after 1 January 1969 (Table 9). In the year 1970, for example, all types of losses totalled 8208 in Lapland of which one-quarter was urban and three-quarters rural.[21]

International emigration from Lapland was second only to Oulu Province in 1970. Lapland led all Finnish provinces during three months and tied for the lead in a fourth. Its maximum losses by international emigration were in August to October of 1970 when 750-900 persons left monthly (Fig. 32). Proportionally these were greater losses than in Oulu Province. Worse yet second highest losses of about 600 each occurred February through April of 1970. Then, as in Oulu and the rest of Finland, there were smaller excesses of out-migration in the fall of 1971.

LAPLAND PROVINCE — MIGRATION NUMBERS

1970—1972

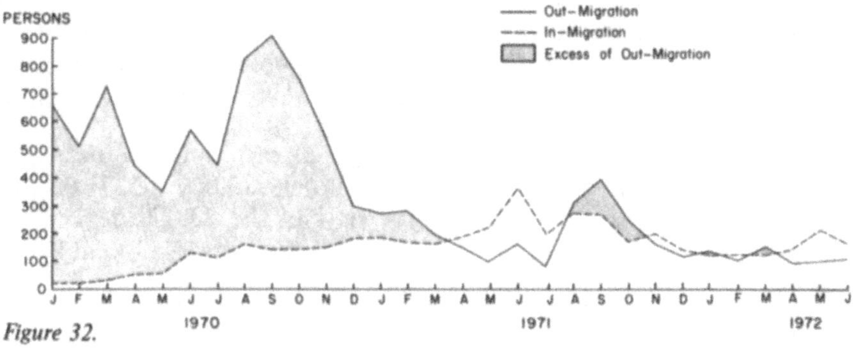

Figure 32.

Unlike the remainder of the country, though, instability of international emigration characterized the first half of 1972. Excess outmigration took place in January and March and in June the inmigrants were only about 50 more than those going out (Fig. 32). A repeat of seasonal losses in the fall of 1972 should not be surprising.

The demographic quality of these figures suggests that stability may be some time, if ever, in developing in Lapland. Majava noted that "A typical emigrant from these counties (Lapland and Oulu Provinces) was an unskilled, single male, aged 17-30 years, coming from a rural commune. Thus, the male population aged 15-29 years was reduced by almost 20 per cent in the rural communes of Lappi (Lapland) in 1969, and in the rural communes of the Oulu county the corresponding figure was 12 per cent".[22] The high 1971 unemployment noted above coupled with reduced farming (from the sponsored slaughtering of cattle and restriction of milk production) may not be adjusted yet; not only may there be further losses directly related to these two items, such as, increasing proportions of older people, but additional reduction of birth rates may be a result of the previous losses in the young-male sector of the province's people.

While Finland adjusts its total economy the internal adjustments of the population may reflect or produce new local or regional problems. And these may be geographic as well as being rooted in other disciplines.

Distributional Changes

A different geography of Finnish population may appear in the near future. In southern Finland it appears likely that the rural agricultural population will become thinner and that some small farms will be abandoned. Cities and towns probably will grow and it is doubtful that there will be major changes in the boundaries of the Region of Continuous Settlement (Fig. 6). However, in northern Finland there is the definite possibility of geographical contraction of the inhabited area toward its present main routes of transportation and principal urban centers (Figs. 7-9).

Recent forecasts of population numbers already appear quite optimistic. Lapland Province's numbers of either 213,000 or 271,000 in the year 2000[23] seem unattainable in view of the 23,000 decline to 197,000 in just the three years following 1 January 1969 (Table 9). This is especially true if places like nearby Kemi decrease to 26,000 and even though Rovaniemi reaches an expected 58,000 by the same year.[24] In fact, birth rates and growth rates in all Finland during recent years point to increases in the total population as being minimal.

In part this is due to the current course of Finland's economy toward more sophisticated industrial production for export. Lapland's contribution to this, on the basis of present inventories and production, is likely to be too indirect for the provincial population to increase. Accelerating hydroelectric production and the supply of raw materials accompanying increasing industrial production has left northern Sweden with regional-scale abandoning.[25] How may Lapland be any different?

It was noted that abandoned farms and vacant homes were not observed in unusually large numbers in Lapland during 1970. Still, colonies like Lisma-aavan, Välijoen, and even Pasmajärven showed distinct signs of sluggishness, if not decline. The lack of sociological and psychological cement in a population is an insidious element of a rural landscape. Further, if it is true that "The contemporary conventional wisdom is to encourage a 'top heavy hierarchy' so that economies of scale can be realised in urban affairs."[26] then dominant cities and towns with lower degrees of regional and local isolations will grow at the expense of other parts of the cultural landscape. Especially will the areas with higher degrees of isolations suffer.

Thereby will Lapland's gains in population from inward rural colonizing be wiped out by outward movements. In fact, they may already have been – and then some. But this reduction in numbers and in inhabited area may be a healthful pruning as was suggested for Sweden.[27]

In any event the colonizing of Lapland was a fruitful experience. The world now has a better record of how to plan for and carry out new rural settling under certain conditions. On the basis of the past this knowledge is valuable because there are always some countries desirous of expanding their inhabited areas for one or more reasons. If new rural settling is to be done it might as well be done as efficiently as possible in our attempts to create a better world.

And in the case of Finland every study is invaluable. The nation at a major interface of two highly contrasting ideologies is worthy of any effort to assure its future.

TABLE 9. Population of Oulu and Lapland Provinces, Finland, 1969-1972

	Oulu		Lapland	
Date	*Total Pop.*	*Rural Pop.*	*Total Pop.*	*Rural Pop.*
31 Dec. 1960[a]	406,992	329,166	205,113	144,999
1 Jan. 1969[b]	422,828	283,386	220,755	148,005
1 July 1970[c]	415,407	247,367	215,230	142,561
1 Dec. 1970[d]	408,429	268,123	209,611	137,443
1 Jan. 1972[e]	397,463	259,177	197,245	128,635

[a] S.V.T., *Yleinen Väestölaskenta, 1960, II,* Helsinki, 1963, p. 4.

[b] Tilastollinen Päätoimisto, *Tilastotiedotus, VÄ 1970: 6,* Helsinki, p. 7.

[c] Tilastollinen Päätoimisto, *Tilastotiedotus, VÄ 1970: 10,* Helsinki, p. 3.

[d] Tilastollinen Päätoimisto, *Tilastotiedotus, VÄ 1971: 2,* Helsinki, p. 4.

[e] Tilastollinen Päätoimisto, *Tilastotiedotus, VÄ 1972: 2,* Helsinki, p. 4.

NOTES TO CHAPTER 5

1. These data have been reported in monthly mimeographed reports from the government's Central Statistical Bureau: Tilastollinen Päätoimisto, *Tilastotiedotus,* Helsinki.

2. Population Reference Bureau, Inc., *1972 World Population Data Sheet,* Washington, 1972.

3. An excellent background to Finland's position as a buffer state is in V. H. Malmström, *Norden: Crossroads of Destiny and Progress,* New York, 1965, pp. 81-97.

4. A. Majava, *Väestönmuutokset Talousalueittain ja Kunnittain Vuosina 1951-1966,* Valtakunnansuunnittelutoimiston Julkaisusarja A:21, Helsinki, 1968, p. 59.

5. A. Majava, Migrations Between Finland and Sweden, in The Scandinavian Demographic Society, *The Second Scandinavian Demographic Symposium,* Stockholm, 1970, pp. 111-118, ref. on p. 118.

6. *ibid.*, p. 116.

7. *ibid.*

8. (World Bank Group), World Bank Atlas, *Finance and Development,* v. 9, 1972, pp. 48-60, ref. on pp. 56-57.

9. A. Majava, The Second...., *op. cit.*, pp. 112-113; V. A. Koiranen, Emigration of Finns to Sweden – Drain or Benefit for Finland, (K-O-P) *Economic Review,* 1970, pp. 47-52.

10. A. Majava, The Second...., *op. cit.*, p. 117.

11. Tilastolinen Päätoimisto, *Tilastotiedotus,* VÄ 1971:2, Helsinki, 24.2.1971, p. 2.

12. G. Beyer, *Rural Migrants in Urban Setting,* The Hague, 1963, pp. 141-152; L. Hautamäki, and P. Viitala, Mechanism of Migration in Finland in the 1960s, *Fennia,* v. 99, No. 7, pp. 1-41; K. Rikkinen, A Circulation Model of Interprovincial Migration in Finland, *Fennia,* v. 99, No. 8, pp. 1-17; L. Hautamäki, Elinkeinon-haarojen sijoittuminen kaupunkija maaseututaajaniin varsinaiselle maaseudulle, *Terra,* v. 78, 1966, pp. 65-71.

13. V. Päävilainen, *National Planning in Finland,* Valtakunnansuunnitelutoimiston Julkaisusarja A:14.3, Helsinki, 1963, p. 12.

14. *ibid.*, pp. 12-13.

15. H. Kärkkäinen, The Structural Change in Distribution in Finland, (K-O-P) *Economic Review,* 1972, pp. 3-13.

16. A. Majava, *Väestönmuutokset....*, *op. cit.*, Cartograms 1-3 (pp. 23-25).

17. U. Kärkkäinen, Drag i utvecklingen av Finlands jordbruk 1959-1969, *Terra,* v. 82, 1970, pp. 147-154; S. Jaatinen and U. Kärkkäinen, *Vuoden 1969 Pellon-varaustoiminta,* Helsingin Yliopiston Maantieteen Laitoksen Julkaisuja, Sarja B, No. 7, Helsinki, 1971.

18. (No author), Economic Development in Finland in 1971, (K-O-P) *Economic Review,* 1972, pp. 14-48, ref. on p. 26.

19. K. Rikkinen, Markov Chain Analysis of Inter-Provincial Migration in Finland, *Fennia,* v. 108, 1971, pp. 1-19, table on p. 19.

20. *ibid.*

21. Tilastolinen Päätoimisto, *op. cit.*, p. 4.

22. A. Majava, Migrations...., *op. cit.*, p. 114.

23. T. Hartman, *Kunnittainen Väestöennuste Vuoteen 2000 Saakka,* Osa I, Helsinki, 1969, p. 37.

24. *ibid.*, p. 66.

25. K. H. Stone, Regional Abandoning of Rural Settlement in Northern Sweden, *Erdkunde,* v. XXV, 1971, pp. 36-51.

26. D. R. Webster, The Effect of Immature Road Networks on the Central Place Hierchy in Frontier Regions, *Terra,* v. 82, pp. 41-46, quotation from p. 46.

27. K. H. Stone, Regional Abandoning...., *op. cit.*, p. 50.

LEGEND TO FIGURES

Fig. 4. High oblique air photograph representative of low local isolation in the Finnish Middle Fringe of Settlement Zone. The predominance of groups of clusters of buildings in a linear area of agriculture and forestry closely attached to a river contrasts sharply with only forests and swamps away from the river. From about 1500 feet above the Kemi River, about 8 miles southwest of Rovaniemi, facing west, on 12 June 1956.

Fig. 5. The Continuous Settlement Region of southern Finland. High oblique air photograph of representative closeness of spacing of residences and lines of transportation. From about 1000 feet elevation, about 23 miles northwest of Helsinki, on 20 August 1964.

Fig. 10. Urriaavan Colony. Air view; the white angular line in the upper left (NW) corner is Route 950 connecting Kuusamo and Salla. Note the "dead end" character of the colony's roads (white lines), the small amount of cleared land in the colony's third year, and the drainage ditches (black angular lines) where hay is now grown. Portion of vertical air photo 5825-122, scale 1/45,000, taken 11 August 1958; published with the permission of the National Board of Survey in Finland.

Fig. 11. Puupuolivarvikkon Colony. Sauna and residence under construction at a new farm, about 18 miles northwest of Salla on 20 July 1960. The sauna served as the residence during the first winter (1959-1960) there for a family of eight persons.

Fig. 12. Pasmajärven Colony. Farmstead in characteristic spruce-birch forested morainic site nine years after the start. Southeast to farm no. 24 on 20 August 1960.

Fig. 13. Pasmajärven Colony. New and old hay fields on characteristic lower drained swamp site. Northwest from farm no. 25 on 15 August 1964.

Fig. 16. Välijoen Colony. Vegetable farm at the break between drained swamp to the left and forested moraine to the right. West at farm no. 35 on 18 July 1960.

Fig. 17. Välijoen Colony. Two-building farmstead of a unit started in 1953, no longer occupied by original settler, and where idle field is largely in fireweed and barn is unoccupied. East to farm no. 23 on 18 July 1970.

Fig. 19. Kapustavuoman Colony. Farmstead at characteristic break between morainic soils and (in distance) swamp soils. Typical well-kept buildings of farmstead with electric power line. Northwest at farm no. 2 on 22 July 1970.

Fig. 20. Kapustavuoman Colony. Air view of the central portion only four years after starting; farm buildings built and herringbone pattern of closely-spaced drainage ditches show settlers' relatively rapid early development. Portion of vertical air photo 5621-241, scale of 1/20,000, taken 3 July 1956; published with the permission of the National Board of Survey in Finland.

Fig. 22. Lisma-aavan Colony. House under construction and temporary barn, with electric power line, and smouldering fires in stump rows on newly cleared morainic soils. West to farm no. 31 on 19 August 1960.

Fig. 23. Lisma-aavan Colony. Completed home and permanent barn, with electric power line and telephone, and continued clearing and burning. West to farm no. 31 on 15 August 1964.

Fig. 24. Lisma-aavan Colony. Air view of the central portion 10 years after the colony's start. Widespread ditching (close black lines) and cropping in the swamps as well as new clearing (light lines) adjoining farmsteads in wooded areas. The school is the large white rectangle at the road junction in the middle of the photo. Portion of vertical air photo 63241-221, scale of 1/22,000, taken July 1963; published with the permission of the National Board of Survey in Finland.

Fig. 25. Lisma-aavan Colony. One of four vacant farmsteads; sauna (on left behind trees) unusable and part of barn roof collapsed. Southwest at farm no. 21 on 17 July 1970.

Fig. 27. Urriaavan Colony. The low relief from the grassy swamp land to the scotch pine on drier ridges. Characteristic Finnish hay cocks of the forage for milk cattle that is produced after ditching. Northeast at farm no. 16 on 18 August 1960.

Fig. 28. Urriaavan Colony. Characteristic fencing and well-kept farmstead of the usual three buildings (with additional garage here) on cleared morainic soils. East to farm no. 13 on 16 July 1970.

Table 4 PASMAJÄRVEN COLONY, started 22 March 1946

Farm No.	No. of Parcels	Arable	AREA (Hectares) Woods	Useless	Total	Est Value 1000 FM[a]	Law Settled Under	Date Agreement Signed	Bought	Cold Farm Prem. (1000 FM) Used by 1960	% of All'w'c'
7	1	20.7	51.2		71.8	85	6[b]	27. 3.50	18. 4.63	63	
8	2	15.4	57.7	7.3	80.5	90	110[c]		30. 4.60	480	53.9
15	1	18.9	83.5	53.7	157.5	114	45WS[d]	24. 9.49	18. 6.63	545	65.4
16	1	29.4	74.6	28.8	132.8	132					
17	2	37.0	78.1	19.3	134.4	100					
18	2	25.8	67.4	15.6	108.9	85	110	5. 4.56	3. 5.62	157	
19	1	25.3	65.2	7.2	97.6	85		5. 4.56	8. 5.62	153	
20	1	19.5	55.8	25.8	101.1	82		17. 6.50	24. 1.60	510	76.6
21	1	18.4	64.0	23.8	106.3	62	45WW[e]	13. 3.51	15. 8.60	540	65.1
22	1	17.7	65.7	9.4	92.7	68	1959[f]	24.10.51			
23	2	21.6	63.2	4.6	89.4	69	6	13. 3.51	24. 3.64		
24	2	19.1	62.4	11.7	93.3	81	45WS	29.11.50	15.11.61	503	79.8
25	2	19.2	65.6	10.4	95.2	72	1959	31. 8.59	21.12.64		
26	2	15.6	68.1	21.9	105.6	75	1959	28. 3.62			
27	2	22.5	69.4	2.8	94.7	77	1959	9. 3.65			
28	2	17.3	64.7	29.2	111.1	97	6	9.11.54	10. 4.64		
EARLIER SETTLERS INCLUDED IN COLONY AREA											
1	3						110			361	
2	2						110			457	
3	2						110			45	
4	2						110			245	
5	1						110			289	
6	1						110				
10 1/2											
11	1						110			177	
12	1						110			484	
26 1/2											
29	1						110				
30	1						110			170	
36	1						110			126	
37	2						110			485	

[a]Price of farm, at the 1944 level, after various possible reductions.

[b]The Land Use Act of 16 Aug. 1958 superseding all prior colonization laws.

[c]A 1936 Settling Law providing no cold farm premium but data in column 11 officially recorded as "Newly Reclaim Land Compensation".

[d]Land Acquisition Act of 5 May 1945, War Soldier Allowance.

[e]Land Acquisition Act of 5 May 1945, War Widow Allowance.

[f]Land Use Act of 1959, allowances generally greater than those of the 1945 Act.

Sources: Data from field observations in 1960, 1964, and 1970, official air photos taken 1954 and 1968; and six official regional offices.

CONSTRUCTION DATES					CONSTRUCTION COSTS (1000 FM)						
House	Barn		Sauna		House		Barn		Sauna		Orig.
Complete	Start	Complete	Start	Complete	Total	Loan	Total	Loan	Total	Loan	S'tl'r
4.11.58					1070	720					✓
20.12.53	16. 7.54				776	500	1150	600			✓
1. 3.57	12. 5.54	12.10.59	. .49	1.10.49	690	450	1150	500	130		✓
7. 8.58	31. 5.58	31. 7.59			980	660	1040	600			✓
8. 5.55	4. 8.54		16. 7.50	4. 5.55	690	450	830	550	168	35	✓
16. 5.55	3.10.54	1. 9.55	8. 8.54	20. 6.55	923	450	940	500	165		✓
				. .60							
		. .63		. .60	1850	800					✓
20. 6.56	4. 7.54		15. 8.51		760	60	1150	700			✓
											✓
	. .64										
											✓
	14. 8.59	19. 5.60			1450	800	1510	600			✓

1970 CHARACTERISTICS

No. Bldgs.	Milk Shed	Milk Platf.	Power Line	Tele- phone	Other
3					House vacant
4	✓				
3					
0					
0					
3		✓			
3		✓			
3					
4		✓		✓	
3	✓				
3		✓			
3					
3		✓			
3		✓			
3					
4		✓			New house just completed
3	✓				
3					
3					House vacant
3					House vacant
2					House not inhabitable
3	✓				House vacant
3					Bldgs. new, barn under construction
4		✓			Replacing old barn
4	✓				
2		✓			Bldgs. new, new clearing to W
3					
3	✓				
4		✓			Milk platform shared with #37
3		✓			

TABLE 5 VÄLIJOEN COLONY, started 14 June 1951

Farm No.	No. of Parcels	AREA (Hectares) Arable	Woods	Useless	Total	Est. Value 1000 FM[a]	Law Settled Under	Date Agreement Signed	Bought	Cold Farm Prem. (1000 FM) Used by 1960	% of All'w'c'	Start
1	3	29.2	129.5	32.3	192.5	416	1959[b]	2.12.60	22.16.65	0		2. 7.
2	3	22.2	96.3	22.7	142.4	302	1959	12.12.60	8.12.65	0		16. 6.
3	3	31.6	137.6	77.2	247.4	542	45WI[c]			95	15.1	
4	2	28.9	158.8	8.4	198.1	373	45WS[d]			20	3.2	
5	2	29.3	141.1	0.1	170.5	337	45WS					
6	2	30.2	147.7	10.7	188.7	438	45WS	17. 3.52	7. 9.61	511	71.0	30. 8.
7	2	29.0	163.0	48.8	240.8	284	45WS	10. 3.52	15. 2.62	469	62.3	10. 7.
8	2	28.2	141.8	23.7	193.6	397	45WI	10. 3.52	31. 7.63	215	34.1	10. 8.
9	2	41.6	135.7	58.6	235.9	340	45WS	10. 3.52	28. 3.62	386	50.3	18. 9.
10	2	42.9	169.1	21.2	233.1	323	45WS	10. 3.52	23.10.62	410	55.6	20. 9.
11	2	25.5	109.2	58.2	192.9	272	1959	26. 8.60	17. 1.66			
12	2	31.8	156.4	70.5	258.7[e]	693	1959	3. 8.62				
12A	1											
13	2	33.5	129.9	39.9	203.3	385	1959	9. 1.61				
14	2	29.0	140.2	11.8	181.0	292	1959	4. 4.60	14. 6.65			
15	2	33.7	165.4	17.6	216.7	569	45WS	9. 6.52	11. 1.60	566	85.9	4. 7.
16	2	33.5	165.1	42.3	240.9	587	45WS	26. 4.54	30. 7.63	620	80.9	28. 7.
17	2	23.3	153.6	28.3	205.1	707	45WS	11. 3.52	22. 7.58	595	88.8	2.10.
18	3	28.1	148.9	25.9	202.9	620	45DP[f]	24. 3.52	10. 2.62	751	82.1	12. 7.
19	2	32.1	149.5	57.9	239.5	725	45WS	19. 5.52	27.10.59	560	81.4	
20	2	27.3	126.4	82.5	236.2	449	45WS	11. 3.52	25.10.60	632	84.8	9. 7.
21	3	26.3	152.8	64.8	243.9	573	45WS	8. 9.52	5.12.60	569	83.4	14. 7.
22	3	22.2	146.4	49.7	218.3	517	45WS	11. 7.55	17. 8.64	540	70.9	2. 7.
23	3	28.8	161.8	43.7	234.3	682	1959	2.11.53	18. 8.64	386	50.6	6. 8.
24	3	20.5	135.8	34.3	209.9	692	45WS	17. 3.52	2.10.59	600	90.4	4. 9.
25	3	31.8	156.8	23.9	232.1	444	45WS	2.10.57	2.10.57	313	39.1	2. 9.
26	3	30.2	158.0	34.7	222.9	522	45WS	11. 3.52	8. 7.59	601	92.9	3.10.
27	3	23.0	125.5	56.9	205.4	463	45WS	11. 7.55	7. 1.64	475	68.6	4. 7.
28	2	21.7	201.9	19.4	243.1	298	45WS	29.11.55	6.10.64	442	57.9	21. 7.
29	2	22.3	145.2	16.8	184.3	668				50	7.9	
30	2	20.8	173.6	33.2	227.6	617	1959	29. 8.60	25.10.65			. .
31	2	22.4	142.5	141.3	306.2	484	45WS	22.11.54	14.11.60	581	84.4	20. 7.
32	2	40.8	159.1	112.6	312.5	500	1959	12. 2.60				
33	1	15.3	107.9	36.1	160.0	481	110[g]		10. 2.60	45		23.10.
34	2	22.5	151.5	23.4	197.4	604	45WS	16. 6.52	17. 8.64	240	38.1	24. 8.
35	2	28.5	145.5	15.4	189.4	691	110		5. 4.60	47		
35A	?											
36	2	24.6	155.3	0.8	180.6	596	45DP	2. 3.53	4. 1.65	402	41.9	10. 7.
37	2	24.0	129.9	75.1	229.0	540	45WS	1. 4.52	3.10.58	597	94.8	2. 9.
38	1	22.6	122.5	45.8	190.9	437	110		18. 5.60	168		21. 9.
39	2	27.4	126.3	66.1	219.8	255	1959	17. 4.61		182		8. 9.
40	2	15.6	135.2	89.9	240.7	445	45WS	3. 3.52	14. 2.62	553	73.1	30. 8.
41	2	31.9	120.6	55.5	208.0	264	45DP	19. 1.53	28. 9.63	418	55.1	10. 8.
42	2	20.3	134.1	16.9	171.2	393	45WS	24.10.52	16. 8.62	553	58.2	3.10.
43	3	30.8	137.9	31.8	199.9	618	45WS	17. 3.52	20. 9.61	632	70.1	18. 7
44	3	30.2	129.0	33.9	193.1	556	45WS	24. 3.52	1.12.59	655	96.2	10. 8
45	2	26.5	149.0	15.8	191.2	623	1959	17. 7.60				
46	3	35.9	152.4	68.2	256.6	601	45WS	11. 3.52	8. 5.62	357	45.7	4.10
47	2	20.6	154.0	128.8	303.3	349	1959	16.12.60				
48	2	37.0	168.9	47.6	250.6	255						
49	2	41.2	149.1	65.1	255.3	410	45WS	26. 1.53	15.12.69	50	6.6	.
50	1	0.6			0.6	17						
51	1	0.8			0.8	7						
52	1	0.9			0.9	7						
53	1	0.7			0.7	7			24. 3.67			
54	1	0.8			0.8	10						
55	1	0.8			0.8	9			30.10.61			
56	1	0.8			0.8	9						
57	1	0.8			0.8	12			30.10.61			
58	1	0.8			0.8	9	1959		24. 4.65			
59	1	0.8			0.8	12						
60	1	0.8			0.8	11			3. 6.64			
61	1	1.2			1.2	28	45WI	17. 3.53	7.11.63			

[a] Price of Farm, at the 1944 level, after various possible reductions.

[b] Land Use Act of 1959, Allowances generally greater than those of the 1945 Act.

[c] Land Acquisition Act of 5 May 1945, War Invalid Allowance.

[d] Land Acquisition Act of 5 May 1945, War Soldier Allowance.

[e] Reduced to 208 Ha. for present (Third) settler; Revised price and areas not available.

[f] Land Acquisition Act of 5 May 1945, Displaced Person Allowance.

[g] A 1936 Settling Law providing no cold farm premium but data in column 11 officially recorded as "Newly Reclaimed Land Compensation".

Sources: Data from field observations in 1960 and 1970, Official Air Photos taken 1959, 1961, and 1967; and six official regional offices.

CONSTRUCTION DATES				CONSTRUCTION COSTS (1000 FM)									
Barn		Sauna		House		Barn		Sauna		Orig.		Milk	
Start	Complete	Start	Complete	Total	Loan	Total	Loan	Total	Loan	S'tl'r	No. Bldgs.	Shed	Pl
		6. 7.56	18. 8.56	1016	400			187			3		
				1200	800						2		
		16. 8.56	6. 9.57	1033	500			184	30		1		
											0		
											0		
7.58				960	500	1098	500	165	0	✓	2		
6.60		10. 7.56	6. 9.56	1150	400	1000	500	184	0	✓	3		
		. .57	11. 8.59	1016	500			268	0	✓	3		
6.60		4. 7.56	20. 8.58	960	425	1100		184	50	✓	4		
6.60		6. 7.56	6. 8.58	960	550	1100		184	50	✓	3	✓	
											0		
											1		
										?	1		
											2		
										✓	3		
		10. 8.56	16. 8.56	960	500	850	500	165	30		3	✓	
8.59		5. 7.56	25. 9.56	1016	500	1060	600	197	40	✓	3		
7.56	12. 3.58	6. 7.53	30.12.55	960	400	940	400	165	30	✓	3	✓	
8.59		8.10.55	30.12.55	960	425		550	165	30	✓	1		
										✓	3		
8.59				1033	550	880	500	165	40	✓	3	✓	
7.56	22. 8.57	2.10.55	30.12.55	960	400	940	425	165	30	✓	3	✓	
7.59		6. 8.55	3.12.55	1033	525	1060	500	268	30	✓	3	✓	
6.60		. .53		1069	450	1000	500	165	0		2		
7.58		18. 7.53	30.12.55	960	500	1098	500		75	✓	3	✓	
.60		. .59		1700	550	1055		600			3		
.57		2. 9.55	30.12.55	960	400	1060	400	165	30	✓	4	✓	
.58		12. 8.55	30.12.55	1033	600	1060	600	268	50		3	✓	
5.60		. .56		1016	500	1055		184	50		2		
				1033	500						0		
				960	450			165			2		
6.57		. .56		1016	400	1060	500	184		✓	2		
				960	400			184			0		
8.55	24. 1.57			750	550	450	270			✓	0		
				1113	500					✓	2		
5.57	. .60					950	565			✓	2		
										?	3		
.59		. .53		1107	600	1100		165	30	✓	2		
8.55	22.11.56	4.10.55	30.12.55	905	450	1098	550	165	35	✓	3		
8.58	4. 1.60			1250	650	520	350			✓	4		
		2.10.55	30.12.55	960	500	926		165			2		
7.59				960	400	1060	500	165		✓	2		
		10. 4.54	18. 6.57	1033	600			165		✓	3	✓	
8.59				940	500	850	400			✓	2		
7.59		6.10.55	20.12.55	1179	400	850	450	165	30	✓	3		
		8.10.52	9. 9.53	1083	500			320	40	✓	3		
											3		
5.60		22. 8.56	18. 5.57	960	450	1430	600	165		✓	3		
											2		
											2		
.59		. .55		1033		2400		184		✓	2		
											1		
											1		
											1		

1970 CHARACTERISTICS

Power Line	Telephone	Other
✓		No Farming ?
		Little Farming ?
		House vacant.
		House vacant, Barn removed.
✓		Little Farming ?
✓		1969 Telephone line not operational, New house under construction
✓		Little Farming ?
✓		
	✓	
	✓	
		No Farming ?
✓	✓	House appearance above average.
✓		
✓	✓	
		House abandoned, barn collapsed.
✓	✓	Little Farming ?
✓	✓	
✓	✓	House appearance above average.
✓		No farming ?
		Barn on field plot in SW.
✓		
✓		
✓		Shares milk platform with 31.
✓		Shares milk platform with 30.
		Buildings moved or dismantled ?
		Buildings moved or dismantled ?
✓		
✓		
✓		Little Farming ?
✓	✓	Little Farming ? One Bldg. moved ?
✓		House appearance above average.
✓	✓	House appearance above average.
✓		No Farming ?
✓		Little Farming ?
✓	✓	
✓		No Farming ?
		No Farming ?
✓		Post Office and Bank in Res., Store separate.
✓		Little Farming ?
✓		
✓		Little Farming ?
		No Farming ? Only 2 Bldgs. ?
		Includes Teacher Residence.
		Also two sheds.

Table 6 KAPUSTAVUOMAN COLONY, started 3 December 1952

Farm No.	No. of Parcels	AREA (Hectares) Arable	Woods	Useless	Total	Est. value 1000 FM[a]	Law Settled Under	Date Agreement Signed	Bought	Cold Farm (1000 F… Used by % … 1960	All
1	3	35.6	107.4	71.7	281.3	662	45WS[b]	20. 9.54	12. 8.59	550	87
2	3	32.0	146.0	28.9	206.9	639	45WS	13. 9.54	17. 4.59	555	84
3	3	39.7	205.3	95.8	340.9	638	45WS	7. 2.55	17.12.58	590	88
4	3	34.0	169.6	57.9	261.6	825	45WS	7. 1.55	12.11.58	593	88
5	3	39.7	146.5	76.1	262.4	678	45WS	6. 7.54	30.12.58	605	90
6	3	39.4	130.8	42.7	212.9	543	45WS	12. 7.54	30.12.58	618	98
7	3	30.6	148.6	55.8	235.0	514	45WS	26. 8.54	10. 6.59	628	93
8	3	35.0	207.6	31.2	273.9	473	45WS	5. 5.54	19. 9.62	600	91
9	3	38.9	131.1	47.8	217.9	538	45WS	12. 4.54	2. 9.60	569	84
10	3	36.1	267.9	36.2	340.1	761	45WS	9. 4.54	27.11.58	606	92
11	2	29.7	226.5	12.7	268.8	670	45WS	9. 4.54	17. 6.60	528	78
12	3	33.7	179.6	46.4	259.7	747	45WI[c]	10. 4.54	27. 2.59		
13	3	36.8	137.9	69.9	244.5	801	45WS	1. 4.54	9. 8.62	503	72
14	3	44.2	220.0	30.6	294.8	581	1959[d]	18.10.64		370	58
15	3	41.8	178.4	47.0	267.2	584	45WS	9. 4.54	24. 2.61	547	81
16	3	45.0	226.1	166.2	437.3	581	45WI	13. 4.54	17. 4.59	561	87
17	2	37.2	186.1	41.7	265.1	912	45WS	10. 4.54	15. 7.59	571	86
18	2	41.2	182.9	25.2	249.3	786	45WS	19. 7.54	18. 2.59	560	81
19	2	40.2	203.6	8.4	252.1	593	45WS	31. 1.55	2. 4.60	575	81
20	2	37.9	189.1	3.1	230.1	490	110[e]		2.10.63		
21	2	27.4	192.1	18.0	237.5	515	45WI	13. 6.55	8. 5.64	442	4
22	3	42.5	183.0	53.7	279.2	575	45WS	6. 6.55	10. 4.61	590	8
23	3	40.4	168.1	72.5	281.0	606	1959		24. 4.63		
24	2	37.3	183.7	129.2	350.2	712	1959		22. 4.63		
25	2	40.1	139.4	128.4	307.9	610	1959		26. 4.63	524	7
26	3	40.1	160.8	134.6	335.5	682	1959		23. 4.63		
27	2	42.7	134.8	68.4	245.9	592	1959		26. 4.63		
28	2	45.9	155.8	109.8	311.5	554	1959		26. 9.63		
29	3	38.8	167.0	28.2	233.9	448	1959		22. 4.63		

[a]Price of farm, at the 1944 level, after various possible reductions.

[b]Land Acquisition Act of 5 May 1945, War Soldier Allowance.

[c]Land Acquisition Act of 5 May 1945, War Invalid Allowance

[d]Land Use Act of 1959, Allowances generally greater than those for the 1945 Act.

[e]A 1936 settling law providing no cold farm premium but data in column 11 officially recorded as "Newly … Land Compensation".

Sources: Data from field observations in 1960 and 1970, official air photos taken in 1956 and 1966, and regional offices.

e	CONSTRUCTION DATES				CONSTRUCTION COSTS (1000 FM)						Orig
	Barn		Sauna		House		Barn		Sauna		
Complete	Start	Complete	Start	Complete	Total	Loan	Total	Loan	Total	Loan	S'ti
15.12.55	10. 6.57	10.11.57	1.11.55	1.12.55	1016	500	1140	600	184	50	✓
15. 9.55	1. 6.57	1.11.57	16. 9.55	1.11.55	950	550	1140	600	184	50	✓
1. 9.55	20. 9.56	25. 9.57	1. 9.55	1.11.55	1250	500	1140	500	184	100	✓
15. 9.55	1. 9.56	15.12.57	10. 5.55	15. 7.55	950	550	1140	550	184	50	✓
	1. 9.56	25. 9.57	10. 5.55	15. 7.55	1016	550	1140	600	184	50	✓
15. 9.55	15. 9.56	20. 9.58	1. 7.56	20. 8.56	1016	550	1150	600	184	50	✓
10.11.55	15. 9.56	25. 9.58	1. 6.55	10. 7.55	1016	550	958	550	184	50	✓
1.12.55	15. 6.57	15.11.58	1. 5.54	15. 8.55	1016	550	1300	500	184	150	✓
1.12.55	10. 9.56	15. 9.58	1. 6.55	15. 8.55	960	550	1140	600	184	50	✓
15.11.54	10. 9.56	15.12.57	15. 9.55	1.12.55	1033	550	1140	600	184	50	✓
20.11.54	15. 9.56		10. 1.55	15.11.55	1033	550	1140	500	184	50	✓
25.11.54	15.10.55	10. 6.58	1.10.55	15. 5.56	965	550	1150	550	184	50	✓
1.12.54	15. 8.56	15.12.59	15. 5.55	1.11.55	960	500	1140	600	197	50	✓
10.12.54	5. 6.55		1.10.55	15.11.55	960	550	1140	500	184	50	
10. 9.56	1. 8.57	15.12.59	15. 6.54	15.11.54	960	550	1300	500	348	200	✓
15.12.55	1. 6.56	20. 6.58	5.10.56	15.12.56	1248	500	1102	500	184	100	✓
15.12.55	1. 9.56	1.12.58	20. 6.54	20.11.54	960	550	1140	600	348	100	✓
15.12.55	20. 9.56	5.12.58	1. 5.55	15. 8.57	1250	550	1140	600	184	50	✓
30.11.56	15. 8.57	25. 9.59	10. 6.55	15.11.55	1250	500	1020	500	184	50	✓
6.11.59					1280	800					✓
15.12.57	15. 6.60		1. 8.56	15. 9.56	1248	600	1020	500	197	50	✓
5.12.56	1. 6.57	1.12.59	1.10.55	15.10.57	1016	550	1020	550	184	50	✓
2.10.58	27. 4.60				1250	800	1400	600			✓
26. 6.58	27. 4.60				980	660	1400	600			✓
2.10.58					980	660					✓
30.10.57					980	660	1280	600			✓
28. 9.59					1070	728					✓
					1070	720					✓
19.11.59	30. 5.60				1070	720	1400	600			✓

1970 CHARACTERISTICS

No. Bldgs.	Milk Shed	Milk Platf.	Power Line	Tele-phone	Other
3		✓	✓		Little farming?
4	✓		✓		
5	✓		✓		
3	✓		✓		
3	✓		✓	✓	
3	✓		✓		
3	✓		✓	✓	
4	✓		✓	✓	
3	✓		✓	✓	
3	✓		✓	✓	
3	✓		✓	✓	
2		✓			Only residence in use?
4			✓	✓	Store in residence
2					Abandoned
3			✓		
4	✓		✓	✓	
4			✓	✓	
4	✓		✓	✓	
3	✓		✓	✓	
3	✓		✓		
3	✓		✓	✓	
3	✓		✓	✓	
3	✓		✓	✓	
5	✓		✓	✓	
2	✓		✓	✓	Shares milk shed with #26
2			✓		Shares milk shed with #25
3	✓		✓	✓	
3		✓	✓		
3		✓	✓		

Table 7 LISMA-AAVAN COLONY: Started 15 May 1953

Farm No.	No. of Parcels	AREA (Hectares) Arable	Woods	Useless	Total	Est. Value 1000 FM[a]	Law Settled Under	Date Agreement Signed	Bought	Cold Farm Prem. (1000 FM)	Used by % of 1960 All'w'c
1											
2	3	32.4	111.3	0.8	144.5	253	P[b]	15. 1.54	7.12.60	620	82.0
3	3	28.1	133.3	17.0	178.4	403	1959[c]	14. 8.63			
4	2	30.5	107.7	1.8	140.0	239	1959	14. 8.61	13.12.67		
5	3	30.6	141.3	27.1	199.1	470	45WS[d]	31. 1.55	27. 1.64	602	93.9
6	3	33.1	159.2	10.8	203.0	656	45WS	15. 1.54	29.10.62	513	79.4
7	3	27.2	191.1	24.7	243.0	164	1959	29. 8.60	22.11.65		
8	2	29.7	162.3	57.6	249.6	408	P-45WS	22. 1.54	24. 1.61	540	85.7
9	3	35.6	147.4	34.0	217.1	397	45WI[e]	14. 1.54	6. 2.62	587	93.2
10	2	26.3	161.7	40.4	228.4	354	P-DP[f]	13. 1.54	25. 1.61	680	89.9
11	2	22.5	154.2	121.6	298.4	233	45WS	17. 5.54	8. 7.65	270	42.9
12	2	22.0	143.3	16.4	181.8	161	1959	25. 8.60	20.10.65		
13	2	30.2	141.9	6.0	178.1	325	45WS	14. 1.54	20. 4.64	550	87.3
14	3	34.8	184.7	8.2	227.7	187	45WS	14. 1.55	19.10.64	415	57.4
15	2	29.5	170.4	24.8	224.8	159	45WS	7. 2.53	10.11.60	620	93.1
16	2	28.5	178.3	6.6	213.4	165	1959	12. 9.60			
17	3	25.9	189.0	2.8	217.7	313	45WS	29. 8.53	14. 2.67	262	32.1
18	2	34.5	194.6	44.8	273.9	113	1959	24. 8.60	22.10.65		
19	3	28.6	183.6	5.8	218.1	294	1959	24. 8.60	1.11.65		
20	2	21.7	175.6	8.9	206.2	149	1959	16.11.60	4. 1.66	557	88.4
21	2	26.6	167.0	0.7	194.3	371	45WS	7. 1.55	25. 4.62	594	84.4
22	3	29.7	160.1	22.8	212.7	268	45WI	31. 1.55	23. 2.65	557	54.3
23	3	23.5	161.5	0.8	185.8	405	45WS	14. 1.54	19.10.64	380	48.8
24	2	29.0	155.2	10.5	194.7	214	45WS	14. 1.54	12. 3.60	597	94.8
25	2	29.1	151.6	0.8	180.9	308	45WS	13. 4.55	9. 3.60	598	94.9
26	2	26.6	179.0	64.0	269.6	230	1959	12. 9.60	22.10.65		
27	2	29.2	169.5	67.9	266.6	297	45WI	2. 5.55	8. 2.61	717	94.8
28	2	33.4	162.4	18.3	214.1	251	45WS	29.11.55	21.10.60	585	91.3
29	2	28.8	153.0	17.3	199.1	436	45WS	2. 4.55	9. 8.62	569	85.7
30	3	26.3	151.5	14.8	192.6	262	45WS	9. 5.55	2. 7.65	561	84.1
31	3	27.3	175.3	20.1	222.7	334	1959	29. 8.60	11. 5.65		
32	3	22.5	139.8	34.7	197.0	358	1959	24. 8.60	14. 7.65		
33	3	30.2	161.2	5.3	195.5	392	45WS	17. 2.55	7. 5.62	585	88.1
34	3	33.5	150.1	19.2	202.8	154	1959	12. 9.60	6. 4.66		
35	2	32.4	194.1	23.1	249.6	217	1959	12. 9.60			
36	2	29.0	145.4	34.1	208.5	301	1959	29. 8.60	2. 8.68		
37	2	25.9	161.6	54.1	241.6	359	1959	21. 8.63			
38	3	36.5	162.8	26.8	226.2	594	45WI	2. 4.54	3. 5.60	710	89.0
39	2	27.4	157.7	0.5	185.6	603	45WS	17. 2.55	5. 4.62	582	87.8
40	3	22.5	195.6	39.2	257.3	291	1959	29. 8.60	30. 9.65		
41	2	28.6	178.2	29.8	234.6	165	1959	24. 8.60			

[a]Price of farm, at the 1944 level, after various possible reductions.

[b]Petsamo District allowances.

[c]Land Use Act of 1959, allowances generally greater than those of the 1945 act.

[d]Land Acquisition Act of 5 May 1945, War Soldier Allowance

[e]Land Acquisition Act of 5 May 1945, War Invalid Allowance

[f]Petsamo District Displaced Person Allowances.

Sources: Data from field observations in 1960, 1964, and 1970, official air photos taken in 1956 and 1963, a six regional offices.

	CONSTRUCTION DATES						CONSTRUCTION COSTS (1000 FM)				
	Barn		Sauna		House		Barn		Sauna		Orig.
mplete	Start	Complete	Start	Complete	Total	Loan	Total	Loan	Total	Loan	S't'l'r
.10.55	15.10.56		1. 6.55	1. 8.55	963	600	1098	600	165	50	✓
					1261	500	730	500			
. 8.56	10. 6.56		10. 6.55	1. 9.55	945	600	1098	675	184	50	✓
.11.55	10. 7.55	30.10.55			1207	650	1514	700			✓
. 8.59					1450	760					✓
. 9.55	1. 6.56		15. 6.54	30. 7.54	967	550	1150	575	165	50	✓
.10.54	1. 7.55	20.10.55	10. 6.54	30. 7.54	965	600	960	600	165	50	✓
.11.55	10. 6.56		20. 6.54	30.10.54	1069	600	1032	600	165	50	✓
			1. 8.58	15. 9.58	1248	650	1140	600	184	50	✓
.10.55	1. 6.54		10. 6.54	15. 7.54	1107	600	1134	500	184	100	✓
.10.54	15. 8.55				892	450	808	500			✓
. 3.57	17. 8.58		20. 9.55	1. 6.56	1107	600	1150	500	184	75	
. 9.59					960	220					
			15. 8.58		1123	500	770		184	75	✓
					960	650					✓
					1200	800					✓
.10.57	15. 6.57		2.10.56	20.10.56	1261	600	1450	650	197	80	✓
			15. 9.55	15.10.56	1107	650	770	450	184	50	✓
					1340	600	1150	600			✓
. 5.56	15. 5.57	15.10.57			1107	600	1134	600			✓
. 7.55	15. 6.56		10. 5.55	15. 7.55	1248	600	1150	600	184	50	✓
. 7.59					1200	800					✓
. 4.56	1.10.56		15. 5.55	1. 9.55	1123	600	2000	150		50	✓
.11.56	1. 6.57	15. 9.58	20. 5.56	23. 6.56	1340	600	1450	650	184	80	✓
.10.55	20. 6.56		10. 6.55	1. 9.55	1123	600	1150	600	184	50	✓
.11.35	20. 6.56		15. 7.55	1. 9.55	1123	650	1150	700	184	50	✓
.11.58					1600	800					✓
					1450	770					✓
. 9.56	15. 6.57		10. 5.55	5.10.55	1123	600	1140	600	184	50	✓
. 6.59					1200	770					✓
. 7.59					1200	800					✓
. 7.59					1450	770					✓
					1120	750					
9.55	1. 6.56	15.11.56			1261	600	1150	590	165	50	✓
.12.56	20. 6.57	15.11.57	10. 6.55	1. 9.55	1123	700	1140	600	184	50	✓
. 8.58					1450	750					✓
					960	640					

1970 CHARACTERISTICS

No. Bldgs.	Milk Shed	Milk Platf.	Power Line	Tele-phone	Other
					Farm never designated
3			✓		Not farming?
2					
3	✓		✓	✓	Newly cleared land.
3			✓	✓	New resid. replaced old.
3			✓	✓	
3			✓	✓	
3			✓	✓	
3			✓		Vacation renters?
2			✓		
3					Farming?
3		✓	✓		
3			✓		Not farming?
2		✓	✓		Resid. vacant; not farming?
3		✓	✓	✓	
2					Resid. vacant, had powerline.
3			✓	✓	
3	✓			✓	
3					Some newly cleared land.
2		✓			Not farming?
3					Resid. vacant, barn and sauna poor.
3			✓		Farming?
3			✓		Farming?
2			✓		Farming?
3			✓		
2			✓		
3			✓	✓	Not farming?
3			✓		Not farming?
3			✓		
2			✓	✓	Adding a building?
3			✓	✓	Farming?
3			✓	✓	
3			✓		
2			✓		Farming?
2			✓		Farming?
3			✓	✓	Farming?
2					Some newly cleared land.
3			✓		
3			✓	✓	
2					Little farming?
0					Farm not developed.

Table 8 URRIAAVAN COLONY, started 25 February 1955

Farm No.	No. of Parcels	AREA (Hectares) Arable	Woods	Useless	Total	Est. Value 1000 FM[a]	Law Settled Under	Date Agreement Signed	Bought	Cold Far (1000 Used by 1960 A1
1	3	28.0	153.6	66.0	247.6	267	45WS[b]	14. 4.55	4.12.63	455
2	3	26.2	168.3	66.5	261.0	282	WD[c]	14. 4.55	10.11.64	460
3	3	28.2	159.1	24.0	211.4	336	45WS	13. 4.55	20.11.62	395
4	3	25.4	141.1	59.0	225.6	275	45WS	13. 4.55	20. 1.64	523
5	3	39.1	147.0	28.4	214.5	297	45WS	13. 4.55	10.11.64	498
6	3	37.1	148.8	50.3	236.2	322	45WS	13. 4.55	10.11.64	495
7	3	26.9	172.8	38.2	237.9	290	45WS	14. 4.55	29.11.63	500
8	3	27.4	145.8	39.8	213.1	277	45WS	13. 4.55	28.11.63	520
9	3	37.4	135.0	31.1	203.6	296	45WS	16. 4.55	21.12.63	415
10	3	21.9	155.1	82.1	259.2	275	45WS	13. 4.55	6. 7.65	475
11	3	31.6	138.6	43.1	213.4	348	45WI[d]	16. 4.55	10.11.64	440
12	3	34.8	124.7	18.2	177.7	377	45WS	15. 4.55	10.11.64	510
13	2	34.6	127.0	24.0	185.5	261	45WI	15. 4.55	20. 1.65	555
14	3	25.1	130.8	33.7	189.6	253	45WS	15. 4.55	10.11.64	480
15	3	27.6	135.1	68.9	231.7	202	45WS	23. 9.57	21. 8.62	515
16	3	31.6	166.8	83.3	280.6	322	45WS	14. 4.55	12. 2.62	535
17	2	44.9	141.4	30.6	216.9	255	45WS	15. 4.55	10.11.64	485
18	3	43.7	109.4	41.8	195.0	276	45WI	15. 4.55	10.11.64	638

[a]Price of farm, at the 1944 level, after various possible reductions.

[b]Land Acquisition Act of 5 May 1945, War Soldier Allowance.

[c]Widow's Allowance

[d]Land Acquisition Act of 5 May 1945, War Invalid Allowance.

Sources: Data from field observations in 1960 and 1970, official air photos taken in 1958, 1963, and 1
six official regional offices.

CONSTRUCTION DATES						CONSTRUCTION COSTS (1000 FM)					
House		Barn		Sauna		House		Barn		Sauna	
t	Complete	Start	Complete	Start	Complete	Total	Loan	Total	Loan	Total	Loan
56	1.10.57	15. 8.58		1. 8.56	15. 6.57	1150	600	845	500	184	50
56	15. 8.58	15. 8.58		15. 8.55	1. 6.56	1152	500	1000	530	184	50
56	1. 6.57	1. 7.59		1. 8.55	30. 6.56	1248	650	1020	500	184	50
55	30.11.56	15. 8.58		1. 7.55	1. 5.56	1248		1020		184	
55	30.11.56	15.10.57		1. 7.55	1. 5.56	1248	650	1020	550	184	50
56	1.11.56	15. 8.58		1.11.55	15. 8.56	1248	675	1020	600	184	50
56	1.11.56	1. 9.58		1.11.55	15. 8.56	1248	675	1020	550	184	50
56	30. 9.56	15. 8.58	15.11.58	15.10.55	15. 7.56	1248	650	1020	550	184	50
56	1.10.57	1. 7.59		10.10.55	15.10.58	1248	650	1020	550	184	50
56	1.11.56	1. 8.58		1. 7.55	1. 8.58	1033	600	1020	550	184	50
56		1.10.59		1. 8.56	15. 9.56	1261	600	1020	500	184	50
56	15.10.57	15. 7.58	15. 8.59	1. 8.56	1. 9.56	1248	600	1020	500	184	50
56	1. 6.58	1. 8.58		1. 7.56	30. 9.56	1248	650	1020	500	184	50
6	30.11.56	1.10.58		1.11.55	1. 9.56	1248	700	1020	550	184	50
8	15.10.58	25. 6.59	15.11.59	1.10.57	1.11.57	1107	650	1020	600	197	40
6	30. 9.56	15. 8.58		15. 8.55	15. 7.56	1248	700	1140	550	184	50
6	30.11.56	15. 7.58	1. 6.59	15. 8.55	15. 6.56	1248	650	1020	550	184	50
6	15.11.56	15. 7.58	15. 6.59	15. 7.55	1. 6.56	1248	650	1082	600	184	50

1970 CHARACTERISTICS

rig. l'r	No. Bldgs.	Shed	Milk Platf.	Power Line	Tele- phone	Other
	3			✓		
	3			✓		Farming?
	3	✓		✓	✓	
	3			✓		
	3	✓		✓	✓	
	3	✓		✓	✓	
	3	✓		✓		
	3	✓		✓		
	3	✓		✓		
	3			✓		Farming?
	3	✓		✓	✓	
	3			✓		
	4			✓		
	3	✓		✓		Resid. vacant.
	3	✓		✓		
	3			✓	✓	
	4			✓		
	4			✓	✓	

GPSR Compliance

The European Union's (EU) General Product Safety Regulation (GPSR) is a set of rules that requires consumer products to be safe and our obligations to ensure this.

If you have any concerns about our products, you can contact us on ProductSafety@springernature.com

In case Publisher is established outside the EU, the EU authorized representative is:

Springer Nature Customer Service Center GmbH
Europaplatz 3
69115 Heidelberg, Germany

Batch number: 10824490

Printed by Printforce, the Netherlands